THE AT•WAR SERIES

M4 SHERMAN
AT WAR

MICHAEL GREEN
JAMES D. BROWN

ZENITH
PRESS

First published in 2007 by Zenith Press, an imprint of MBI Publishing Company, Galtier Plaza, Suite 200, 380 Jackson Street, St. Paul, MN 55101-3885 USA

Zenith Press titles are also available at discounts in bulk quantity for industrial or sales-promotional use. For details write to Special Sales Manager at MBI Publishing Company, Galtier Plaza, Suite 200, 380 Jackson Street, St. Paul, MN 55101-3885 USA.

Library of Congress Cataloging-in-Publication Data

Green, Michael, 1952-
  M4 Sherman at war / Michael Green and James D. Brown.
    p. cm.
  ISBN-13: 978-0-7603-2784-5 (softbound)
  ISBN-10: 0-7603-2784-X (softbound)
  1. Sherman tank. 2. World War, 1939-1945—Tank warfare. I. Brown, James D. II. Title.
UG446.5.G695 2007
940.54'173—dc22
                            2006021414

Editor: Steve Gansen
Designer: Kou Lor

Printed in China

On the cover, main: In the collection of the Virginia Museum of Military Vehicles is this fully restored M4A3 tank. *Michael Green*

   Inset: This M4 tank is shown taking cover in the fall foliage during a training exercise conducted at Fort Knox, Kentucky. *Patton Museum*

On the back cover: On a training exercise in the United States is this M4A1 tank carrying a small group of infantrymen posing for the cameraman. *Patton Museum*

On the frontispiece: Here is the business end of a 76mm gun mounted on a second-generation M4A3(76)W. *Patton Museum*

On the title pages: Taking part in the Patton Museum of Cavalry and Armor's annual 4th of July living history show is this nicely restored M4A3(105) equipped with the VVSS system. *Chun Lun Hsu*

About the authors
Michael Green is a freelance writer, researcher, and photographer who specializes in military, transportation, and law enforcement subjects, with more than fifty books to his credit. In addition, he has written numerous articles for a variety of national and international military-related magazines. He resides in northern California.

James D. Brown served twenty years in the U.S. Army as an armor officer, with secondary specialty in research and development. His active duty service includes a four-year tour as an assistant professor of engineering at the United States Military Academy, where he taught combat vehicle design and automotive engineering.

CONTENTS

ACKNOWLEDGMENTS

BESIDES THOSE MENTIONED IN THE TEXT OF THIS WORK, the authors would like to thank a number of individuals for their help in the completion of this book. These include Gladys Morales, Bill Nahmens, David Marian, Randy Talbot, Jim Lewis, David Fletcher, Richard Cox, Ron Hare, Dean and Nancy Kleffman, Rick Griest, Carey Erickson, Allan Cors, Don Moriarty, James Warford, Larry Tucker, Candace Fuller, Marc Sehring, Mark Singer, Bob and Trish Fleming, and Jacques Littlefield.

Institutions that assisted the authors include the Military Vehicle Technology Foundation, the Patton Museum of Cavalry and Armor, the Tank Museum in Bovington, England, and the Tank Automotive and Armaments Command (TACOM).

Seeking some additional protection from German AP projectiles, the crew members of this second-generation M4A3(76)W HVSS have welded on additional armor plate to the front of their tank's hull that extends all the way down to cover the cast armor differential housing. A nonstandard pintle for a .30-caliber machine gun is also fitted in front of the tank commander's cupola. *Patton Museum*

INTRODUCTION

THE M4 SERIES, POPULARLY REFERRED TO AS THE "SHERMAN" TANK, is the best-known American tank ever built. Its iconic stature is preserved even in modern society, where millions of laymen still recognize only two types of tanks—water tanks and Sherman tanks. With almost 50,000 produced between 1942 and 1945, the M4 series tank served in almost every part of the globe during World War II. Not only did this mass-produced vehicle equip the armored formations of the U.S. Army and Marine Corps, but it also saw service with a whole host of Allied armies, including the Free French, Russian, Indian, Canadian, New Zealand, Polish, and British.

The name Sherman came from the British. In a departure from its usual naming convention, during World War II the British Army nicknamed all American-built tanks in its inventory after famous American Civil War generals, memorializing Grant, Lee, and Stuart, as well as Sherman. Hence, the modified M3 medium tank supplied to the British in the early days of the war received the name General Grant. When the British Army received the M4 series of tanks, it nicknamed it the "General Sherman." Most tankers dropped the General part and decided to call the tank the Sherman, or the M4 (regardless what model of the M4 series they were using).

During the war years, the M4 series proved to be a study in contrasts. The American public saw this tank as an invincible land battleship dashing around battlefields, blowing up or running over anything that stood in its path. For many American and Allied tankers, the view from inside the tank looking out was not a pretty one. Underarmored and undergunned when compared with late-war German tanks, it was also easy prey to a wide variety of German antitank weapons, ranging from handheld rocket launchers to towed antitank guns.

When the M4 series first saw combat in 1942 with the British Army in North Africa, it was considered almost on par with the leading edge of tank technology. Yet, by the time the invasion of Europe began in June 1944, the M4 series seemed outdated when fighting German tanks.

The reason for this sudden inequality had numerous roots. Foremost was the U.S. Army doctrine that stressed the role of the M4 series as an exploitation vehicle, not as one designed to engage in combat with enemy tanks. The doctrine held that the antitank mission should be left to specialized tank destroyers. Almost as important was an early decision to capitalize on the United States' geographic position as an industrial base that was secure from direct enemy action, and thus it could win the war by out-producing the Axis powers.

The relatively decentralized American heavy-industrial base allowed economies of scale in both new production and repair parts, providing that a standardized design could be set. The Americans decided that the enemy could be defeated by sheer weight of numbers, rather than by seeking cutting-edge technology. Combat experience in the war later proved this doctrine to be seriously flawed. The attempts at making the M4 series tanks viable combat vehicles were hampered by too many people being involved in the process. Various organizations within the U.S. Army interpreted the results of combat experience and intelligence data on enemy weapon systems differently.

During the war, the Germans and Russians engaged in a tank technology race. The Americans, who lacked experience in large-scale tank warfare between 1942 and mid-1944, were seriously handicapped by comparison. While the German and Russian armies were engaging in massive tank battles involving thousands of tanks on either side, the U.S. Army in North Africa, and later in Italy, never saw more than a hundred enemy tanks at any one time.

Back in the United States, four main players worked together to design and develop the M4 series. The Army Ground Forces (AGF) decided what type of tank the U.S. Army needed and specified testing. The Armored Board performed operational tests on the tank's suitability in mobility, firepower, and maintainability, although these tests were not usually carried out in a tactical context. The Ordnance Department performed the engineering testing of prototype tanks developed by civilian contractors, and had contracting authority for production. Finally, yet importantly, individual generals exercised personal prerogatives, often based on their experiences in earlier wars fought in their young and impressionable years.

The AGF could never figure out what it wanted in a tank. It therefore fell upon the officers of the Ordnance Department to come up with tank and weapon concepts. While many of its ideas proved to be promising, much of what the Ordnance Department attempted during the war came from seat-of-the-pants deductions and gut feelings instead of scientific analysis and combat unit inputs. This method of tank development led to constant quarrels that effectively delayed the fielding of an M4 series replacement (i.e. the M26 Pershing) until the closing months of the war.

The success that the U.S. Army achieved with the M4 series tanks during World War II was more due to American and Allied air superiority and artillery support than any distinguishing element of the tank's design. In the end, the quantity of M4 series tanks, rather than their quality, overwhelmed the German war machine.

The design philosophy, which led to an easily producible, readily maintainable, and flexible design, was not entirely without merit. Not until the mid-1950s, when the Israel Defense Forces began to upgrade its imported M4 series tanks with improved guns and engines, did many realize the soundness and great flexibility of the vehicle's design. In the numerous wars that Israel fought against its Arab neighbors, the M4 series tanks—upgraded by Israel and crewed by better-trained tankers—constantly bested newer post-war tanks that the Soviet Union supplied to its Arab allies.

This book is not intended to be a complete combat or technical history of the M4 series tank. Considering the scope of the tank's use since 1942, that would require a multivolume series well beyond the goals of the authors and publisher. Instead, the authors present an overview of the American military gun-armed versions of the M4 series that saw combat from World War II to the Korean War. We hope that the book may provide for the reader a feeling of what it would be like to be a member of an M4 tank crew.

This picture shows the experimental medium tank T5E2 armed with a short-barrel low-velocity 75mm howitzer in a limited traverse mount, which is installed on the right side of the vehicle's hull. The protrusions on either side of the small box-like turret are the armored tubes that contain an optical rangefinder. Besides the main armament, the vehicle mounted five .30-caliber machine guns. *Patton Museum*

On display at the U.S. Army Ordnance Museum at Aberdeen Proving Ground, Maryland, is this beautifully restored example of an early version of the Panzerkampfwagen (Pz.Kpfw.) IV. Armed with the original short-barrel low-velocity 75mm howitzer, the tank appears in the color and markings of the German Army formations that served in North Africa between 1941 and 1943. *Richard Isner*

CHAPTER ONE

M4 BACKGROUND

ON SEPTEMBER 1, 1939, THE GERMAN ARMY, led by over two thousand tanks, swept across the Polish border and began what would later be recognized as the opening action of World War II. While the mainstay of the German tank fleet consisted of light tanks armed with nothing larger than a 20mm automatic cannon, there were also two hundred Panzerkampfwagen (Pz.Kpfw.) IV medium tanks fitted with short-barrel turret-mounted 75mm howitzers on the battlefield. The British and American armies gave the Pz.Kpfw. IV the designation Mark IV, whose appearance on the battlefields of Europe had a dramatic effect on future American tank design.

The U.S. Army had been spending most of its time and money on the development of light tanks, though it did not completely neglect developing medium tanks in the period between World War I and World War II. A number of design concepts were explored; however, none were judged successful enough to place into production until the late 1930s.

In late 1936, the U.S. Army's Ordnance Department recommended development of the five-man T5 medium tank (the "T" standing for experimental), using the proven suspension system design of the army's M2 light tank. (The letter "M" indicated a weapon or vehicle approved for production.) In order to determine the best mixture of weapons to mount on the 15-ton T5, a large number of configurations were proposed. Most included a combination of machine guns and at least one turret-mounted 37mm main gun. One T5 configuration that showed promise was a modified short-barrel 75mm howitzer at the front of the hull, with very limited traverse. The same vehicle, now designated the T5E2, also featured a small one-man turret armed only with a .30-caliber machine gun.

The T5 received power from a Continental air-cooled gasoline-powered radial engine. This modified aircraft engine sat in the rear of the vehicle, and developed 268 horsepower at 2,400 rpm. The engine transmitted power to the tracks through a multiple disc clutch via a long driveshaft, which bisected the bottom of the hull to a constant mesh transmission at the front of the tank. This basic layout of a rear-mounted engine allowed for the protection of the vulnerable grilles—required for cooling airflow—while the front-mounted transmission and clutch was the simplest

The largest armament of the M2A1 consisted of a long-barrel high-velocity turret-mounted 37mm gun, designated the M3. Besides the 37mm gun, the M2A1 mounted eight .30-caliber machine guns. Two were in fixed forward-firing positions in the front hull, four more were in the hull installed in limited-traverse mounts, and the last two were the coaxial machine gun and one on a flex mount on top of the turrent for antiaircraft protection. *Patton Museum*

means to communicate driver hand and foot motions to the transmission, steering, and brakes.

With war clouds looming in Europe in early 1939, prior to the German attacks on Poland in late 1939 and France in the summer of 1940, the U.S. Army decided to produce a version of the T5 armed with a turret-mounted 37mm main gun and eight machine guns. Called the M2 medium tank, production started in the summer of 1939 with eighteen authorized for that fiscal year and another fifty-four for the following year. Tests conducted with the early-production M2s led the army to order a number of improvements for the 1940 production vehicles. Reflecting these changes, the vehicle was designated the M2A1 medium tank.

Retired Major General Gladeon M. Barnes, the chief of the U.S. Army Research and Ordnance Department

during World War II, describes in "History of Tank Development by Ordnance Department in World War" (June 12, 1951), the gasoline-powered M2A1 medium tank: "This was the type of tank which was desired by the infantry at that time. I might say that this was before the formation of the Armored Services and at that time, the tank was considered primarily an infantry weapon. The M2A1 tank carried a 37mm gun in the turret and as I remember, some six machine guns. The 37mm gun was thought of as an antitank gun to protect the tank against other tanks but the real purpose of the tank at the time was thought of as a machine gun nest."

Due to the successful German military invasion and conquest of France and the Low Countries in May 1940, spearheaded by tanks like the Pz.Kpfw. IV, the American government authorized sufficient funding for the U.S. Army to rebuild itself into a force strong enough to defend the nation's interests. Among the many items of military equipment, the army felt a fleet of modern medium tanks, to supplement the light tanks already in series production, would be of crucial importance for the future.

M3 MEDIUM TANK

On August 15, 1940, the U.S. Army entered into a contract with Chrysler Corporation for the production of one thousand units of the M2A1 tank. The terms of the contract called for the order's completion by August of 1942. Only thirteen days later, reports from overseas indicated that the M2A1 tank was already obsolete by European standards, so the U.S. Army immediately ordered that production cease.

In July 1940, production resumed on an equal number of tanks, designated the M3. Design work on the new medium tank, the building of a full-scale wooden mock-up, and the construction of the first pilot vehicle took place between August 1940 and January 1941.

Powered by a Wright air-cooled gasoline radial engine, the 21-ton M2A1 had a maximum speed of 26 miles per hour on level ground. Constructed of face-hardened armor riveted and bolted together, the maximum armor thickness on the tank was 1 1/8 inches on the front of the differential housing. The top of the hull was 3/8 inch thick, and the bottom of the hull was 1/4 inch thick. *Patton Museum*

Parked side-by-side is an M2A1 medium tank and the mockup for the M3 medium tank. The main armament of the new M3 consisted of a right-front-hull-mounted short-barrel low-velocity 75mm gun with limited traverse, and a long-barrel high-velocity turret-mounted 37mm gun. *Patton Museum*

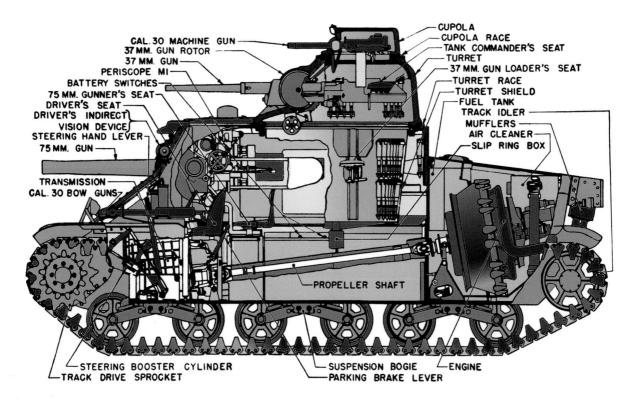

CAL. 30 MACHINE GUN
37 MM. GUN ROTOR
37 MM. GUN
PERISCOPE MI
BATTERY SWITCHES
75 MM. GUNNER'S SEAT
DRIVER'S SEAT
DRIVER'S INDIRECT
VISION DEVICE
STEERING HAND LEVER
75 MM. GUN

TRANSMISSION
CAL. 30 BOW GUNS

CUPOLA
CUPOLA RACE
TANK COMMANDER'S SEAT
TURRET
37 MM. GUN LOADER'S SEAT
TURRET RACE
TURRET SHIELD
FUEL TANK
TRACK IDLER
MUFFLERS
AIR CLEANER
SLIP RING BOX

PROPELLER SHAFT

STEERING BOOSTER CYLINDER
TRACK DRIVE SPROCKET
SUSPENSION BOGIE
PARKING BRAKE LEVER
ENGINE

A line drawing of an M3A4 tank illustrates both a host of interior and exterior components of the vehicle. Notice how the crankshaft height of the tall radial engine necessitated use of the angled propeller shaft running from the rear of the vehicle to its front. This forced the turret basket higher and in turn raised the height of the tank to an unacceptable level. *James D. Brown*

While Chrysler was tooling up for the building of the M3, the U.S. Army still had a pressing need for training tanks and thus awarded a contact to Rock Island Arsenal for 126 units of the M2A1. Only 94 were built before the U.S. Army cancelled the contract in August 1941, as the first batch of M3s rolled off the assembly lines.

In a July 25, 1943, Ordnance Department report, Brigadier General John K. Christmas describes the early decision-making process on the design layout of the new M3 medium tank:

A meeting was arranged at Aberdeen Proving Ground, Maryland, in August 1940, between General Chaffee, the Chief of the Armored Force, and his representatives, and representatives of the Chief of Ordnance, to decide upon the characteristics for the new medium tank which was to be put into quantity production. As an outcome of this meeting, it was agreed to build a medium tank with heavier armor than the Medium Tank, M2, and also mounting a

75mm gun. The preliminary studies of this tank, which had already been made prior to the meeting, indicated the ultimate desirability of mounting the 75mm gun in a main turret having all around fire, but due to the necessity for early production . . . it was decided to proceed at once with the design having the 75mm gun in the right sponson [hull]. It was agreed that a design having a 75mm gun in the main turret was to come afterwards.

Completion of the final design work on the M3 tank took place in early 1941. By the summer of 1941, full-scale production began and continued until August 1942 with 4,924 units built. At first, the M3 called for a crew complement of seven men. That number later dropped to six when the U.S. Army decided that the driver could double as the tank's radioman, as the radio was inside the vehicle's hull near the driver.

Not everyone believed that the M3 was worth building in large numbers. The senior leadership of the U.S. Army's new Armored Force (formed in July 1940)

In this dramatically composed picture, an M3 tank can been seen with its crew members aiming their various self-defense small arms—including the well-known Thompson submachine gun—at an imaginary enemy. Due to a shortage of M1911 automatic pistols, some soldiers were issued .45 revolvers early in the war. *Library of Congress*

suggested that no more than a few hundred M3s should be built until a turret large enough to house a 75mm main gun was designed and constructed.

Due to the pressing need of the British Army in North Africa for American-built medium tanks, the Ordnance Department wanted to continue M3 production, despite objections from others within the military. One objection came from General Adna R. Chaffee Jr., the first commander of the U.S. Army Armored Force. He described the M3 as having "barely satisfactory performance characteristics."

M3 POWERPLANTS

The original M3 production was followed by 1,334 tanks built in five slightly different configurations, designated M3A1 through M3A5. The M3, M3A1, and M3A2 received power from a modified gasoline Wright (later Continental) air-cooled aircraft radial engine.

An advantage of air-cooled engines for tank designers was elimination of the plumbing intricacies and extra weight of water-cooled engines, yet the disadvantages were numerous. Test engineers at Aberdeen Proving Ground, Maryland—the home of the U.S. Army Ordnance School—stated in a January 14, 1942, report, "The engine as presently installed is definitely underpowered. Improvements to this installation have increased the horsepower available but the HP/Wt [horsepower to weight] ratio is

still too low to give completely satisfactory performance." Reports from army training exercises in which the M3 took part also indicated that the radial engine was, "unsatisfactory as to performance and life." Some officers of the Proof Department at Aberdeen recommended that "additional consideration be given to other power plants with a view to increasing the HP/Wt ratio as well as improving the accessibility."

An early production M3 is crossing a trench in this photograph. The M3 series could cross a 7.5-foot-wide trench and climb over a vertical wall 24 inches high. The short-barrel low-velocity front-hull-mounted 75mm gun on the tank could fire a 15-pound armor-piercing (AP) projectile with a muzzle velocity of 1,930 feet per second. *Patton Museum*

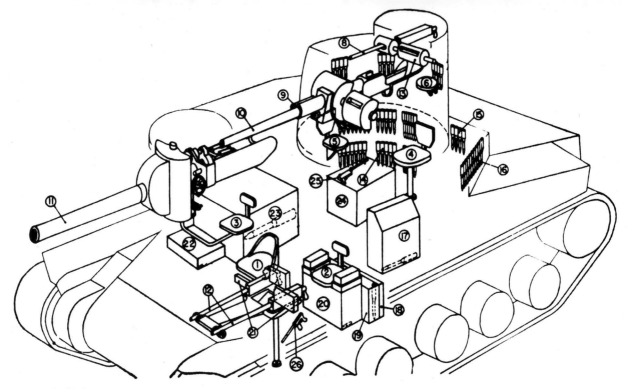

1. Driver's seat.
2. Radio operator's seat.
3. 75-mm gunner's seat.
4. 37-mm gunner's seat.
5. 37-mm gun loader's seat.
6. Tank commander's seat.
8. Cal. .30 machine gun.
9. Cal. .30 machine gun.
10. 37-mm gun.
11. 75-mm gun.
12. 2 cal. .30 machine guns.
13. Protectoscopes.
14. 51 rounds 37-mm ammunition carried in turret.
15. 13 rounds 37-mm ammunition.
16. 11 rounds 37-mm ammunition.
17. 42 rounds 37-mm ammunition.

18. Ten 100-round belts cal. .30 ammunition.
19. 20 rounds 37-mm ammunition.
20. Fourteen 250-round belts containing 225 rounds cal. .30 ammunition.
21. Two 250-round belts containing 225 rounds cal. .30 ammunition.
22. Twenty-five 100-round belts cal. .30 ammunition.
23. 41 rounds 75-mm ammunition; six 100-round belts cal. .30 ammunition.
24. 42 rounds 37-mm ammunition.
25. Submachine gun.
26. Submachine gun. Carried in tank but not shown on drawing are 9 rounds 75-mm ammunition carried in cartons and twenty-four 50-round clips cal. .45 ammunition.

Visible in this ghosted line drawing of an M3 tank is the stowage location of the ammunition for both the turret-mounted 37mm gun and the hull-mounted 75mm gun. Also appearing is the stowage locations for the various small arms carried onboard and the seat locations for some of the crew. *James D. Brown*

Despite having more than enough funding in 1942 to develop a suitable tank engine for the M3, it was clear to all within the U.S. Army that to delay M3 medium tank production until the perfect engine was available was not realistic. So, despite its shortcomings, the air-cooled gasoline-powered radial engine would remain in many American medium tanks throughout World War II.

A further disadvantage of the radial engine was that it was inherently tall and its crankshaft was also higher above the engine bay floor than a comparable inline or V-type engine. The overall engine bay height drove the

height of the turret ring (and hence the hull height). The high driveline affected the turret basket design, because the driveline had to pass beneath the turret to the front-mounted transmission.

The lack of a suitable tank engine for the M3 was not the fault of the Ordnance Department, as it had foreseen this requirement long before the M3 entered U.S. Army service. During the 1930s, however, money for such projects was not available within the U.S. Army's budget. Civilian industry had little interest in developing a specially designed engine that had no commercial applications.

This M3A5 belongs to a private collector. The 37mm gun in the tank's turret fired a 2-pound projectile, with a muzzle velocity of 2,000 feet per second. The M3A5 could attain a maximum speed of 30 miles per hour on level roads for short periods. Normal operating speed was 25 miles per hour on level roads. *Michael Green*

Because there were insufficient numbers of radial air-cooled gasoline-powered engines for the U.S. Army's medium tanks, and since the U.S. Army Air Forces required the same engine for many of its training aircraft, the U.S. Army decided to employ a modified twin commercial General Motors (GM) liquid-cooled diesel-powered truck engine in its M3A3 and M3A5 tanks. This engine joined at its fan ends with a heavy junction plate and at the flywheel ends with a double clutch housing. A transfer unit then transmitted power to a single propeller shaft. The drivers of the tanks had a single pedal that provided uniform engagement between the two clutches via an adjustable linkage.

If one engine went down, the driver had clutch lock-out cables leading to the instrument panels. These cables allowed him to disengage either engine in case of a failure, so that the surviving engine could operate without the drag of the other. On paved level roads, the twin diesel engines of the M3A3 and M3A5 provided the vehicles a top speed of 30 miles per hour, while on a single engine a top speed of 20 miles per hour was possible.

Between December 1941 and April 1942 at Aberdeen Proving Ground, tests were conducted between gasoline-powered M3 series tanks and those with the twin diesel-powered engine arrangement and showed the advantages of the latter engine. An Ordnance Department report from 1942 states the following regarding the twin diesel-powered engine arrangement: "The power plant has very good performance. Mileage and cruising range are better than those with gasoline engines. The cooling and starting characteristics of these engines are equal to or better than those of the standard production M3 tanks."

Another improvised engine arrangement for the M3 series coupled five Chrysler commercial liquid-cooled gasoline-powered truck engines in a star-shaped assembly around a single driveshaft. Referred to as the Chrysler A-57 Multibank, this massive powerplant required lengthening the M3 hull by more than a foot. To compensate for the increase in vehicle length and weight, the designers also enlarged the spacing between the center and rear bogie assemblies of the suspension system. The modified vehicle was designated the M3A4.

U.S. Army tests of the A-57 Multibank in October 1942 demonstrated that it furnished adequate power for the M3A4 tank. However, continual minor failures made maintenance very difficult. Nonetheless, Chrysler received a contract to build 109 units of the M3A4, all of

On display at Aberdeen Proving Ground, Maryland, is an M3A1 with a cast armor hull. The side door in the vehicle's hull was a serious ballistic weak spot in the tank's armor and disappeared from late production vehicles. Early vehicles had their national recognition symbols (star) and identification stripes painted in yellow. In later vehicles, these markings were white. *Michael Green*

The specially designed turret on the M3 Grant—as can be seen on this beautifully restored M3 Grant—provided room for a radio in its rear bustle for the tank commander to operate. This was a British Army requirement. In the U.S. Army version of this tank with a much smaller turret, the radio was located in the front hull and operated by a radioman. *Michael Green*

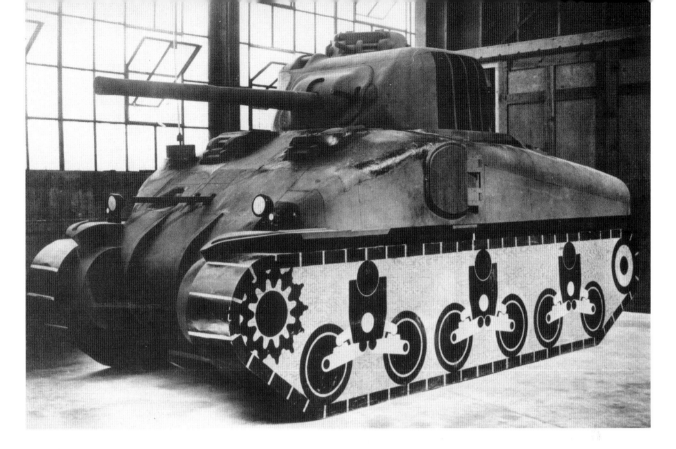

Pictured on display at Aberdeen Proving Ground in August 1941 is the medium tank T6 wooden mockup. In June 1941, Aberdeen received the go-ahead to build a complete operational pilot tank with a cast hull, and it first ran in September 1941. The tank commander's cupola seen on the wooden mockup did not make it into the operational pilot tank. The fixed bow-mounted machine guns were carried over from M2 and M3. *Patton Museum*

which remained in the United States as training vehicles. The gross power of the M3A4 with the A-57 Multibank powerplant was 425 horsepower at 2,850 rpm. The maximum net horsepower for the tank topped out at 370 horsepower at 2,400 rpm.

M3 ARMOR PROTECTION

Prior to the design and building of the M3 series of medium tank, U.S. Army tanks employed face-hardened armor in their construction. A description of this type of armor appears in a September 1950 U.S. Army report titled "The Vulnerability of Armored Vehicles to Ballistic Attack," which states, "Face-hardened armor is characterized by an extremely hard face surface with a relatively soft back. . . . The advantage of using face-hardened armor is in its ability to break up attacking projectiles striking its hard surface, thereby greatly reducing their ability to penetrate. . . . It is more difficult to manufacture than homogeneous armor, since carburizing necessitates heating in a furnace for a considerable period of time. . . . Because of these difficulties of manufacture, face-hardened armor is rather expensive and cannot be produced in comparable tonnages to homogeneous armor." For these reasons, the Ord-

nance Department decided to use only homogeneous armor for the M3 series in June 1940.

Homogeneous armor is essentially uniformly hard throughout its depth and has a very high degree of ductility (the property of a material that allows it to withstand large amounts of deformation before fracturing). It is therefore not only easier and more cost-effective to manufacture than face-hardened armor, but also lends itself much more easily to machining and arc welding. Another positive quality of homogeneous armor is toughness, which is the ability to absorb energy without deformation or fracture. Sheet lead is very ductile, but does not make good armor because it lacks toughness.

A major factor that had swung the Ordnance Department in favor of homogenous armor over face-hardened armor for its M3 medium tanks emerged in a series of firing tests at Aberdeen Proving Ground. These tests showed if homogenous armor was properly sloped, it had resistance to penetration almost equal to face-hardened armor.

The M3A1 featured a cast homogeneous armor (CHA) upper hull and a riveted lower hull. The decision to use CHA in the upper hull was due to the successful

This is a side view of the T6 operational pilot tank built by Aberdeen Proving Ground. To speed up its design and assembly, as many components as possible were borrowed from its predecessor, the M3 series. Armored Forces officials requested the elimination of the armored doors on either side of the vehicle's hull. *Patton Museum*

use of CHA in the turrets of the M3 series. Firing tests conducted with early production units of the M3A1 at Aberdeen Proving Ground showed excellent results and led to the Ordnance Department approving the construction of CHA upper hulls as an alternate for the M3 series. However, the main problem was an insufficient number of foundries capable of making the large casting for the M3A1, which forced the Ordnance Department to use other methods.

On the M3 and M3A4, the upper and lower hull consisted of rolled homogeneous armor (RHA) plates riveted together. While welded construction was far superior, especially for armor, the American factories building the M3 and M3A4 were more familiar with the tried-and-proven process of riveting and offered to build riveted hulls much faster.

The disadvantages of riveted RHA armor soon became apparent in test firings conducted at Aberdeen Proving Ground, which occurred shortly after the Japanese attack on Pearl Harbor in December 1941. These tests showed that "heavy machine gun fire drove rivets into the fighting compartments of tanks and there created a hazard fully as lethal as shell fragments. Furthermore, bullet splash entered through riveted joints, and, under the impact of armor-piercing projectiles as small as 37-mm, the joints parted at the seams. Although some of these shortcomings were corrected in ways such as welding rivet heads to the interiors of vehicles, the greater strength of welded joints as well as the time saved in production soon led to the wholesale adoption of welding."

Since the M3 and M3A4 went into production before the attack on Pearl Harbor, there was no way for the Ord-

nance Department to change the manufacturing process without upsetting the very high production rate demanded by President Franklin D. Roosevelt. The Ordnance Department did the next best thing and had subsequent models of the M3 series use RHA arc welded together in their construction.

Cast CHA armor was more popular than plate armor with the manufacturers, since it avoided the fabrication problems of welding thick sections of armor steel plates with ballistic-quality arc welds. Another big advantage of CHA was that the manufacturers could vary the thickness over a large given area. For this reason, CHA has historically been used in the construction of tank turrets and

This picture of the T6 operational pilot tank without its upper cast hull shows the arrangement of the vehicle's lower hull, with the seats for the driver and assistant driver. Also evident is the drivetrain that runs from the rear of the vehicle to the front-mounted transmission. *Patton Museum*

Pictured is the second production unit of the M4A1 tank, which came with the name "Michael" on its side in honor of British citizen Michael Dewar, head of the British Purchasing Commission in the United States. It resides on display today in the Tank Museum, Bovington Camp, Dorset, England. *Patton Museum*

mantlets (rotor shields) whose complex shapes require different protection levels in various locations. A disadvantage of CHA is that it must be thicker and heavier because it lacks the toughness added by the work-hardening process of rolled homogeneous armor.

RHA is easier to produce in large quantities and welds easily. It also offers superior protection when struck by antitank projectiles due to its toughness. RHA also protects well against the shockwaves generated by large-caliber projectiles striking the exterior of a tank's armor and the blast from high-explosive rounds. A disadvantage of RHA is its inability to form easily. Because of this, manufacturing of complex shapes requires many small flat plates, which raises manufacturing costs.

M3 ARMAMENT

All versions of the M3 in American military service featured a power-operated CHA turret armed with the 37mm M6 gun and a coaxial M1919A4 .30-caliber machine gun. A small CHA cupola with two vision ports was armed with an M1919A4 .30-caliber machine gun and sat on top of the turret.

The 37mm guns mounted in the M3 series turrets were fitted with elevation gyrostabilizers, which allowed for firing on the move. The crews of the M3s could rapidly engage targets ranging anywhere from 200 to 700 yards in any direction. Lack of azimuth stabilization made the shoot-on-the-move capability more theoretical than practical. However, the psychological advantage of being able to return fire while seeking a covered firing position encouraged crews not to halt in the open when fired upon, and hence was perhaps worth the effort. Other armies did not agree, and stabilization was not to be seen on any tanks other than American ones in World War II.

In his book titled *Sherman: A History of the American Medium Tank*, Dick Hunnicutt describes the 75mm guns mounted in the front hull of the M3 series:

Main armament of the first pilot M3 was the 75mm gun T7 number 1. This was the modified version of the 75mm gun T6 retaining its bore length of 84 inches. It was chambered to use the standard 75mm ammunition issued for the 75mm gun M1897. The latter was the French 75 adopted by the U.S. during World War I. With a slightly shorter barrel, the muzzle velocity of the T7 was 1850 ft/sec [feet per second] compared to 1950 ft/sec for the field gun. Initially, the 75 was considered as support artillery and not as the primary antitank weapon, so there was little or no concern about muzzle velocity or armor

An early production M4A1 tank featured the direct-vision slots for the driver and assistant driver, as well as three .30-caliber machine guns (two fixed and one in a flex mount) mounted in the front hull. This tank also had a sight rotor on the top front of the tank's turret, soon replaced by the M4 periscope that included a telescope sight within it. *Patton Museum*

piercing performance. In fact, experiments were carried out shortening the barrel to 71.25 inches, but the muzzle blast was considered excessive so the 84-inch length was retained. Equipped with a semi-automatic vertical sliding breechblock, the T7 was standardized as the 75mm gun M2.

From the start, a longer barrel 75mm gun had been planned for the M3. It had a bore length of 110.63 inches and featured a semiautomatic breechblock. The longer barrel of the 75mm gun M3 boasted a muzzle velocity of 2,030 feet per second with the same ammunition used in the shorter 75mm gun M2. Like the turret-mounted 37mm gun on the M3, the 75mm gun in the front of the hull was gyrostabilized in elevation. Traverse on the 75mm guns was no more than 30 degrees (15 degrees to either side).

In addition to the 75mm gun in the M3 series front hull, there were also two .30-caliber machine guns to be operated by the driver. This feature was a design vestige, which had also appeared in the M2 and M2A1 medium tanks. These guns reflected the battlefield environment of World War I, where tanks were intended to negotiate the infantry-infested barbed wire entanglements of No Man's Land, by sweeping the ground ahead of them clear with un-aimed machine gun fire.

On a training exercise in the United States is this M4A1 tank carrying a small group of infantrymen posing for the cameraman. The white strip around the turret of the tank pictured is for identification purposes, in order to prevent friendly-fire incidents. The M4A1 disappeared from use in early 1943. The blue strip under the white strip was to denote the opposing sides in war games. *Patton Museum*

Posing for its official portrait is an M4A1 tank. Standing on one side is a soldier to provide a perspective of its size and height. Missing from this tank is the tow cable that normally extended from the rear of the vehicle's hull to the front of the hull. Two cables were required to tow a tank, so each tank carried one cable. *Patton Museum*

BRITISH ARMY VERSIONS OF THE M3

The British Army lost the bulk of its tanks during the evacuation at Dunkirk (France) in the summer of 1940. Since British industry could not mass-produce new tanks to replace its losses, the British government had to purchase directly from the American manufacturers. It ordered one thousand M3 series with a specially designed CHA 37mm turret large enough to contain a radio set in the rear bustle for operation by the tank loader.

The British CHA turret for the M3 series lacked the U.S. Army's machine-gun-armed cupola. In its place, the British Army had installed a circular split-cover hatch that reduced the vehicle's height by 4 inches. American-style M3 tanks in the service of the British Fourteenth Army in Burma were converted to the British Army version by retrofitting the same type of split-cover circular hatch.

The British Army designated its version of the M3 series as the "General Grant I." The M3A5 with the American-designed turret and machine gun cupola was

The rear engine doors of an M4A1 tank are shown in this photograph. Also visible are the two circular air cleaners located on either side of the engine doors. Just above the engine doors are the two muffler tail pipes, while at the bottom of the lower hull are tow points. *Patton Museum*

On display at Fort Hood, Texas, is an M4A1 tank. On level roads, it could attain a top speed of 24 miles per hour for short periods. The tank had a maximum operational range, with a full fuel load on level roads, of approximately 120 miles. Operating off-road could cut the maximum operational range to less than half. *Michael Green*

the "General Grant II." Other versions of the M3 series with the original machine-gun-armed cupola went by the name "General Lee" with a different Roman numeral to distinguish various models.

THE COMBAT DEBUT OF THE M3 SERIES

The British Army M3s first saw action in North Africa on May 27, 1942, when the German Army launched an attack on British Army tank units stationed near the small desert town of Bir Hacheim. The 75mm gun on the M3 tanks outranged the short-barrel 75mm howitzers on the German Army Pz.Kpfw. IVs, while the armor protection on the front of the vehicle's hull and turret proved nearly impervious to many of the German tank and antitank gun munitions.

U.S. Army units first saw action with M3s on November 28, 1942, when American and British ground forces took control of a small town and an airfield in Tunisia, North Africa, from German forces. During the attack, the tank crews of the American M3s suffered heavy losses from hidden German antitank guns. Over the next few days, the American tankers suffered additional losses at the hands of the more experienced Germans.

The M3 tank had a number of design shortcomings, including the vehicle's 10-foot height. The limited traverse of the hull-mounted gun meant the entire tank had to turn to engage an enemy vehicle in almost any direction except head-on.

Because the 75mm gun in the M3 series sat so low in the front hull of the vehicle, it was impossible to fire the weapon without exposing the entire tank to enemy observation and return fire. Since more powerful German tank guns were taking a heavy toll on the M3s in North Africa, the army was anxious to field a new medium tank as quickly as possible.

BEGINNINGS OF THE M4 MEDIUM TANK

On August 31, 1940, the Armored Force Board released detailed characteristics for a new medium tank armed with a turret-mounted 75mm gun. Six months later, the Chief of Ordnance requested that Aberdeen Proving Ground proceed with the design of the new tank following completion of upgrade work on the M3 tank series. The Chief of Ordnance directed that automotive features of the new medium tank—including the air-cooled gasoline-powered radial powerplant, powertrain, suspension, and track—should be essentially those of the M3 medium tank.

The principal change was moving the hull-mounted 75mm gun into a turret. Also agreed upon was the use of welded RHA or CHA hulls. Increasing the thickness of the vehicle's armor, while at the same time reducing the number of crew members, was also considered an important goal in order to up-armor the tank without increasing the vehicles' gross weight.

In June 1941, the Ordnance Committee ordered the building of a full-size wooden mockup and a pilot model of the new tank designated the T6. Upon completion of the wooden mockup, followed by a few design changes, Aberdeen Proving Ground started to manufacture a complete pilot tank with a CHA hull and turret. Rock Island Arsenal started building a pilot tank with a welded RHA hull. The turret would come later, as the turret design was not yet ready for production.

Aberdeen Proving Ground rolled out its 30-ton T6 pilot tank on September 2, 1941. After representatives of the Armored Force and the Ordnance Department inspected the new tank, two major changes were ordered. The first was to replace the ballistically inferior side escape doors with an escape hatch in the floor just behind the assistant driver's position. The second was to eliminate the .30-caliber machine gun CHA cupola from the top of the vehicle's new turret.

On September 5, 1941, the Ordnance Committee ordered production of the M4 medium tank. Just one month later, the characteristics were amended to add a

The box-like welded hull of an M4 tank, which presented a large easily penetrated target to enemy antitank gunners, is clearly visible in this staged photograph of a crew loading a variety of weapons into this vehicle, including main gun rounds and hand grenades. *Patton Museum*

Coming out of a U.S. Navy Landing Ship Tank are a couple of M4 tanks, with spare track links affixed to their front hulls. The tank in the foreground has steel tracks. The tanks belong to the 1st Armored Division and are coming ashore at Anzio on May 23, 1944, to take part on the advance on Rome, Italy. *Patton Museum*

.50-caliber antiaircraft machine gun on the top of the tank turret. Another change was to fit a .30-caliber gun in a ball mount, which would be operated by the assistant driver, in the vehicle's front hull. Finally, two fixed forward-firing .30-caliber machine guns, which would be operated by the driver, were to be mounted in the front hull. A directive issued in March 1942 soon dropped the hull-mounted guns from the design.

NEW DESIGNATIONS

By November 1941, the manufacture of M4 pilot tanks had begun. In December, the Ordnance Committee designated the welded-hull versions as M4 and designated the cast hull versions as M4A1. Aberdeen Proving Ground used the pilot T6 (by now an M4A1) for further development.

In British Army service, the M4 became the Sherman I, and the M4A1 became the Sherman II. Although the name Sherman did not come from the U.S. Army, it did become popular with many U.S. Army tankers fighting in Europe during World War II and shows up in army reports from the period. In the decades after the war and to this day, it has remained its primary name.

Some M4 series crewmembers called their vehicles the "M4" or just the "medium." Tom Sator, a loader on an M4 series tank in Northwest Europe during World War II, remembers calling them either a "75" or "76," based on the size of the main gun mounted on the vehicle. When the officers were not around, Tom said the crews often referred to their tanks as "rolling steel coffins."

In late 1941, the U.S. Army's main concern was that there was no interruption in the production of tanks when the changeover from the M3 to the M4 series took place. The Ordnance Department took delivery of the first series production cast-hull M4A1 from the Lima

Removed from a long-forgotten military target range and still bearing the marks of numerous hits is this composite-hull M4, which features the combination of a rear three-quarter welded hull, mated together with the front end of a cast-hull M4A1. *Chris Hughes*

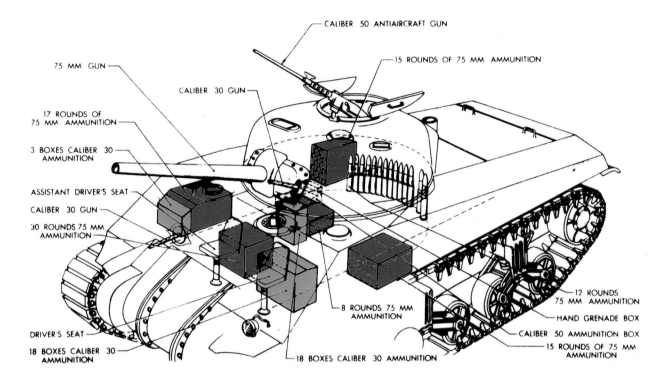

CALIBER 50 ANTIAIRCRAFT GUN

15 ROUNDS OF 75 MM AMMUNITION

75 MM GUN

CALIBER 30 GUN

17 ROUNDS OF 75 MM AMMUNITION

3 BOXES CALIBER 30 AMMUNITION

ASSISTANT DRIVER'S SEAT

CALIBER 30 GUN

30 ROUNDS 75 MM AMMUNITION

DRIVER'S SEAT

18 BOXES CALIBER 30 AMMUNITION

8 ROUNDS 75 MM AMMUNITION

18 BOXES CALIBER 30 AMMUNITION

12 ROUNDS 75 MM AMMUNITION

HAND GRENADE BOX

CALIBER 50 AMMUNITION BOX

15 ROUNDS OF 75 MM AMMUNITION

This ghosted line drawing of a welded-hull M4A4 series tank shows the ammunition storage arrangement for both the 75mm main gun rounds and the ammunition for the vehicle's three machine guns. With their vertical hull sides, the welded-hull M4 series tanks could carry ninety-seven main gun rounds, in comparison to the ninety in the cast hull M4 series tanks. *James D. Brown*

Locomotive Works in February 1942. The second vehicle went to Great Britain, bearing the name "Michael" in all capital letters on its side, in honor of Michael Dewar, head of the British Tank Mission in the United States. This shipment was influenced by the U.S. government's cancellation of a British order for four hundred M3 medium tanks so that Lima could build more M4A1s.

In March 1942, the Pressed Steel Car Company started building M4A1s, with Pacific Car and Foundry Company starting in May of that same year. Production of the M4A1 would continue at the three firms until December 1943, with 6,281 units built.

In July 1942, the Pressed Steel Car Company started production of M4s. Four other manufacturers soon joined in, including Baldwin Locomotive Works, the American Locomotive Company, the Pullman Standard Car Company, and the Detroit Tank Arsenal.

Near the end of its production run of M4s, the Detroit Tank Arsenal combined a CHA front hull with a RHA rear hull. Many describe this hybrid hull arrangement as the composite variant.

Due to a lack of radial engines, the Ordnance Department began exploring other engine options for the M4 series. One arrangement involved the mounting of the same twin diesel engines and powertrain that had appeared in the M3A3 and M3A5 medium tanks into a welded-hull M4 tank. Reflecting the changes to the tank's design, it was designated the M4A2; the pilot model is shown here. *Patton Museum*

This late production M4A2 tank features the welded-hull components such as the driver and assistant driver's hatch hoods, bow machine gun port, turret ring guards, and antenna socket mount next to the assistant driver hatch hood. All of these components began appearing on the tank in the fall of 1943. Earlier versions of the tank had the cast armor counterparts of these components. *Patton Museum*

M4 AND M4A1 DIFFERENCES

Other than a few minor differences resulting from the welded upper hull design of the M4, the M4A1 was almost identical to it, with the same engines, power-trains, and suspensions. Due to the more angular shape of the M4, it had room for ninety-seven rounds of 75mm main gun ammunition versus only ninety rounds of main gun ammunition in the more rounded hull of the M4A1.

In the original welded-hull M4 tank, the ninety-seven main-gun rounds were divided between the turret and hull. Twelve vertically orientated rounds were arranged around a raised step on the lower turret basket wall, with another eight stored horizontally in a ready rack on the turret basket floor underneath the main-gun breech mechanism. Behind the loader's seat in the left sponson (the horizontal hull plate that overhangs the track) were fifteen main-gun rounds stored horizontally.

Two opposing sets of storage racks were located on the right sponson. The front-most rack contained seventeen main-gun rounds stored horizontally. The rear rack contained fifteen main-gun rounds also stored horizontally. Another thirty rounds were stored in a horizontally orientated storage rack underneath the turret basket floor, accessible only by the assistant driver.

The ammunition storage arrangement for the cast-hull M4A1 differed only in the number of main-gun rounds stored on the left sponson storage rack. Instead of the twelve main-gun rounds in the welded-hull M4 tank, the M4A1 had room for only eight main-gun rounds.

NEW ENGINES

As with the M3 series, the lack of enough air-cooled gasoline-powered radial engines proved to be a serious problem for the M4 series. The Ordnance Department was forced to use whatever motive power was available.

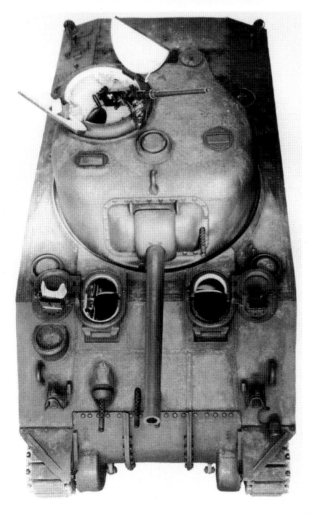

This overhead picture of an M4A2 tank clearly shows the narrowness of the hatch openings for the driver and assistant driver. To enter or exit these hatches required twisting the body sideways, which could be a serious obstacle for a wounded crewman. *Patton Museum*

The Ordnance Department took the twin liquid-cooled GM diesel engines installed in the M3A3 and M3A5 and stuck them in a welded-hull M4. Reflecting various modifications made to the tank—primarily in the engine compartment—it was designated the M4A2. Production began in April 1942 at a number of different manufacturers and continued until May 1944, with 6,748 units built armed with the 75mm main gun. In British Army service, the M4A2 became the Sherman III.

In March 1942, the U.S. War Department issued a policy stating that only gasoline-powered M4 series tanks would go overseas to American forces. Diesel-powered M4 series tanks were for training purposes within the United States only, or for supplying to Allied nations also fighting the Axis. Despite this ban on sending the M4A2 overseas with American fighting men, when the Marine Corps initially requested M4 series

tanks, it ended up with about two hundred M4A2s in late 1943.

M4A3 TANK

The only practical substitute for air-cooled radial engines proved to be the Ford GAA liquid-cooled gasoline-powered engine. The Ordnance Department installed it in a welded-hull M4 and designated the tank the M4A3. In outward appearance, the M4A3 differed from others in the series only in its rear engine compartment arrangement and some other minor features.

The eight-cylinder Ford GAA was an experimental aircraft engine with high output power for its size and weight. Maximum gross power was 500 horsepower at 2,600 rpm. The net power as installed in the M4A3 was 450 horsepower at 2,600 rpm.

If sufficient production capacity had existed for the Ford GAA engine, the Ordnance Department would have replaced the air-cooled radial engine across the entire M4 fleet. However, not everybody was convinced the Ford GAA was the perfect solution. According to Captain Charles B. Kelly of the 2nd Armored Division in a wartime report, "the Ford engine is considered very good," he writes, but then adds, "if you'd add two more cylinders you'd have an engine."

Production of the M4A3 began at Ford in June 1943 and continued until September 1944, with 1,690 units built armed with the 75mm main gun. As with the M4 and M4A1, the M4A3 weighed about 33 tons. It first entered service with the U.S. Army unit in the European Theater of Operations (ETO) in the summer of 1944, and soon became the preferred M4 series tank due to its superior engine. By the end of the war in Europe, almost half the army's inventory of tanks consisted of some version of the M4A3 tanks. It entered into Marine Corps service in late 1944.

The British Army received only seven M4A3 armed with the 75mm main gun from the United States. The British used them only as test vehicles and designated them the Sherman IV.

Skip Warvel, curator of the Indiana Military Museum, compares the radial engine to the Ford GAA engine in the M4A3 tank: "With a Ford V8, you can put it in second gear and start at idle speed, no problem. If you try that in a radial, nine times out of ten, you'll kill it. It just doesn't have the power to move 62,500 pounds forward at idle. So, from a driving standpoint, it's much easier to drive the Ford engine than the radial engine."

This army illustration shows a cutaway view of an M4A2 tank powered by two diesel engines. Other than the ones the Marine Corps received and some retained in the United States for training purposes, most of these diesel-powered M4 series tanks went off to America's wartime allies. *Patton Museum*

THE M4A4 TANK

Desperation also drove the Ordnance Department to okay the mounting and installation of an improved version of the M3A4's Chrysler A57 Multibank gasoline-powered engine into welded-hull M4 series tanks. Like the M3A4, the large and bulkier powerplant mandated a lengthened hull and suspension system. Ordnance Department tests showed the A57 Multibank was the least satisfactory of the engines selected for the M4 series and recommended that when a sufficient number of other types of engines became available, its production would come to an end.

With no interest in the A57 Multibank version—designated the M4A4—except for stateside training purposes, the American army decided to provide most of them to the British Army, as had been done with the M3A4 tank.

According to author David Fletcher in his book titled *The Universal Tank: British Armour in the Second World War Part 2,* automotive engineers from the British Tank Engine Mission looked with absolute horror on the A-57 Multibank–powered tanks being offered to it. He writes, "Even so, Britain took most of the 7,500 M4A4s built before production ceased in September 1943 (including 1,400 originally allocated to the U.S. Army for training) and found them to be quite serviceable if one overlooked the maintenance difficulties. Indeed it probably accorded well with the British temperament to make a virtue from trying to get the best out of the worst possible engine."

In British military service, the M4A4 became the Sherman V. Chrysler completed 7,499 units between July 1942 and September 1943. The lengthening of the M4A4 and the larger and heavier powerplant drove the vehicle's weight to almost 35 tons.

Due to a serious U.S. Army shortage of M4 series tanks during the Battle of the Bulge (December 1944 to January 1945), the British Army returned a number of M4A2 and M4A4 tanks to the U.S. Army. Most went on to see service with the American Third Army, under the command of General George S. Patton.

THE M4A6 TANK

The only other M4 series tank to see the mounting of an alternate powerplant was the composite hull M4A6. It featured a Caterpillar Tractor Company modification of a Wright G200 air-cooled, gasoline-powered radial turned into a diesel engine with a fuel injection system. Originally referred to as the Caterpillar D200A, it later became the Ordnance Engine RD-1820, denoting a radial diesel with displacement of 1,820 ci. Unlike the other engines in the M4 series, the new powerplant in the M4A6 could operate on variety of petroleum products ranging from crude oil to gasoline, making it the first example of a multifuel tank powerplant.

Chrysler began production of the M4A6 in October 1943. However, the Ordnance Department decided to discontinue production in February 1944 after only seventy-five units were completed. The cancellation was

In the collection of the Virginia Museum of Military Vehicles is this fully restored M4A3 tank. The M4A3 was the preferred version of the M4 series in U.S. Army service because of its Ford GAA gasoline engine, which provided an excellent power-to-weight ratio compared to other M4 series tank engines. It also had the advantage of high output and compactness. *Michael Green*

based on changing military requirements and a decision to concentrate on building more of the gasoline-powered M4A3 tanks.

All of the M4A6 tanks came with the same unusual combination of a cast-hull front mated to a rear three-quarter-welded hull, as did some late production M4 tanks built at the Detroit Tank Arsenal and labeled the composite variant.

M4 SERIES COMBAT DEBUT

Like the M3 series, the M4 series would see its first combat action in North Africa with the British Army. In September 1942, during the Battle at El Alamein, a small detachment of German Army medium tanks ran into the 2nd Armored Brigade, which was just recently supplied with the M4 series tanks. After a brief engagement that left several tanks burning on both sides, the German Army tanks withdrew.

After the Battle of El Alamein, the number of M4 series tanks in British Army armored units increased so dramatically that it soon became its most widely used and highly regarded type in service. A statement from a senior British Army officer that showed up in a U.S. Army report, titled "Tankers in Tunisia," asserts, "In my

This postwar picture show an M4A3 taking part in opposing forces training, as evident from the modified uniforms worn by the crew. An external spotting feature at the rear of the hull of the M4A3 is the large flat piece of armor plate, which reached down to the bottom hull of the vehicle and the wide engine exhaust grills arrangement just below it. *National Archives*

The fate of so many M4 series tanks was to become monuments scattered across this country and other parts of the world. This particular M4A3 tank is on public display in Ohio. The eight-cylinder gasoline engine put into the M4A3 tank came from design work done by Ford on an experimental aircraft engine with two cylinders. *Jim Mesko*

opinion the Sherman is the finest tank in the world, better than anything else we have and also better than anything the Germans have. It will be the best tank for the next five years."

The very confident U.S. Army suffered its first defeat with the M4 series in North Africa in December 1942. In an inauspicious beginning, a platoon of five tanks from the 2nd Armored Division went up in flames from a combination of accurate German tank and antitank gunfire. This same scenario took place a couple of months later on a much larger scale, when the German Army punched a hole through American II Corps' lines and inflicted terrible losses in both men and equipment. More than one hundred American tanks, most of them M4 series, littered the barren North African battlefield in its aftermath.

Lieutenant Colonel L. V. Hightower, the executive officer of the 1st Armored Regiment of the 1st Armored Division, which took such a drubbing from the German Army, explains in an after-action report how the Germans prevailed in that series of encounters: "Generally they try to suck you into an antitank trap. Their light tanks will bait you in by playing around just outside effective range. When you start after them, they turn tail and draw you in within range of their 88s. First, they open up on you with their guns in depth. Then when you try to flank them, you find yourself under fire of carefully concealed guns at a shorter range. We've just got to learn to pick those guns up before closing in on them."

Lieutenant Colonel E. A. Russell Jr., also an executive officer of the 1st Armored Division, in a June 10, 1943 report, says about one of the problems that plagued

An overhead photograph of an M4A3 tank shows the upper rear-hull details that distinguished it from other M4 series tanks. Also visible in the photograph are the two circular upper-hull plate ventilators and the single ventilator on the turret roof. *Patton Museum*

The third pilot version of the M4A4 tank posed for its official photograph at Aberdeen Proving Ground in May 1942. The five modified gasoline car engines joined together and referred to as the Chrysler A57 Multibank engine powered the M4A4. *Patton Museum*

the U.S. Army during its time in North Africa—that of over-confidence:

In the initial stages of the operation of this command in November and December 1942, such over-confidence resulted in the rapid whittling down of a medium tank battalion [fifty-three tanks] to less than twenty tanks within a few minutes of actual combat. Another incident: shortly afterward a platoon of M4 replacement tanks with new crews, upon being assigned a mission and given warning of the effect of enemy fire against the M3s, charged gloriously but vainly up a hill only to lose four of five tanks from AT [antitank fire].

Talking to the platoon leader afterwards he truthfully explained that, one he was confident that present AT guns were ineffective against the new M4 and two, that his method of approach was based on an approved solution given under similar circumstances on maneuvers.

Despite their losses in North Africa, most American tankers considered the M4 series a fine tank and more than sufficient for any job at hand. From a U.S. Army report comes this quote from a Sergeant Becker, who saw combat in North Africa: "I like the M4. I look at the German tank and thank God I am in an M4."

Differences in design philosophy are very evident in this picture showing the silhouettes of a Russian T34/76 medium tank and one of its American counterparts, the M4A4 tank. The diesel-powered Russian tank was lower, faster, and better armed and armored than M4A4 tank. The T34/76 also appeared in production before the M4 series tanks did. *Patton Museum*

The M4A1 tank was a bit over 19 feet long, 8.6 feet wide, and 9 feet high over the tank commander's overhead hatch cover. Combat-loaded with a full load of fuel and ammunition, the tank weighed just a bit over 33 tons. Maximum speed of the M4A1 tank for short bursts on level roads was 24 miles per hour. *Michael Green*

This M4 tank is shown taking cover in the fall foliage during a training exercise conducted at Fort Knox, Kentucky. The armor on the upper and lower front hull of the vehicle was 2 inches thick, with the upper front hull plate being sloped at 56 degrees. *Patton Museum*

CHAPTER TWO
DESCRIPTION

AN IDEAL TANK WOULD CARRY ARMOR SUFFICIENT to protect against enemy fire from any direction. However, the design process for a real tank must consider the overall weight of the vehicle, so compromises must be reached. The usual design practice is to distribute armor based on where enemy fire will most likely hit the tank. Normally, the thickest armor is on the front hull of a tank, with progressively thinner armor running along the sides and rear of the hull. The upper and lower front hull on the standard M4 series tank was 2 inches thick, while its sides and rear were 1 1/2 inches thick. Armor on the top of the hull was only 3/4 inches thick. The armor thickness on the floor of the tank ranged from 1 inch in the very front to only 1/2 inch at the rear.

Tank designers normally aim for making their hulls as small as possible to reduce weight and exterior dimensions. Weight reduction is an obvious goal, not only for bridge and road carrying capacity, but for the less obvious effects on engine power requirement and fuel consumption. Height and width are considerations not only for strategic mobility (i.e., ease of getting the tank to the battlefield), but also for tactical mobility (i.e., ability to pass through narrow streets, overpasses, and other restricted terrain). The problem for the designers is to retain enough room in the hull of a tank for the crew and weapons to function properly and for the vehicle's powerplant, powertrain, ammunition, and other operating equipment, while also keeping the overall weight and height of the tank to a minimum.

HULL

Located within the left front hull of the M4 series tank was the driver, with the vehicle transmission to his right. The differential, steering brakes, and final drives were integrated in a housing that was bolted directly to the transmission and extended across the entire width of the hull in front of the driver's knees.

An April 1945 U.S. Army manual describes the duties of the driver: "The driver must be trained in notifying the gun crew when he is about to cross obstacles and rough terrain or turn sharply. He should be competent to maneuver the tank into the most favorable position for the gun crew to fire, and to hold the tank on a straight, even course when firing is done on the move."

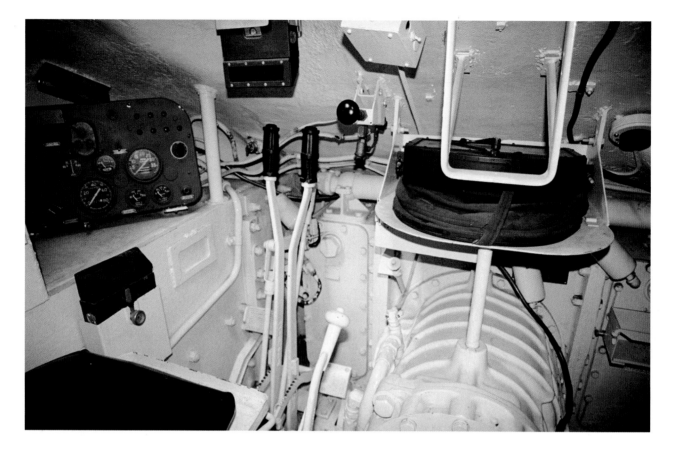

Visible in this picture taken from the turret basket floor of an M4A1 tank is the driver's position. On his left is the driver's instrument panel, while the two steering brake levers are located in front of his seat and the transmission is to his right. Just above the transmission is the storage tray for the driver's foul weather hatch hood. *Michael Green*

On the right side of the transmission sat the assistant driver (also known as the bow gunner). Despite his title, this crew member did not have any driving controls, and his presence was principally to add a fifth crew member to assist in maintenance and round-the-clock security of the tank during extended combat. His presence also added flexibility to crew assignments in case of injury or loss of another crew member.

The assistant driver operated the M1919A4 .30-caliber machine gun fitted in a flexible ball mount directly in front of him. The weapon was secured to the interior front hull in a bracket mount. The mount did not have an aperture for sighting, so the assistant driver could only aim the bow gun by observing his tracer rounds through his hull-mounted fixed-vision blocks, and then directing his fire to the chosen target.

Both the driver and assistant driver on the M4 series had form-fitting padded seats with padded backrests. The seats were fitted with detachable backrests, mounted

on pedestals that were adjustable for height, as well as backward and forward movement. Electrically operated ventilating blowers located in the upper hull plate provided some relief from gases generated during weapons firing. There was also a dome light for the driver and assistant driver.

The driver and assistant driver entered and left the vehicle through spring-balanced overhead armored hatches, each containing a periscope in a mount set on a ball-bearing race, which allowed 360-degree rotation. They could hold the periscopes in any position desired by tightening the rotation set screw, and its mount could tilt 30 degrees up or down. A large nut on the back of the periscope held it in its mount, and a safety lock prevented the periscope from falling out if the nut became loose.

For operating the vehicle in the rain or snow with the hatch open, the drivers on M4 series tanks were supposed to have had a hatch hood—essentially a mini-convertible top of plexiglass and canvas. The hoods

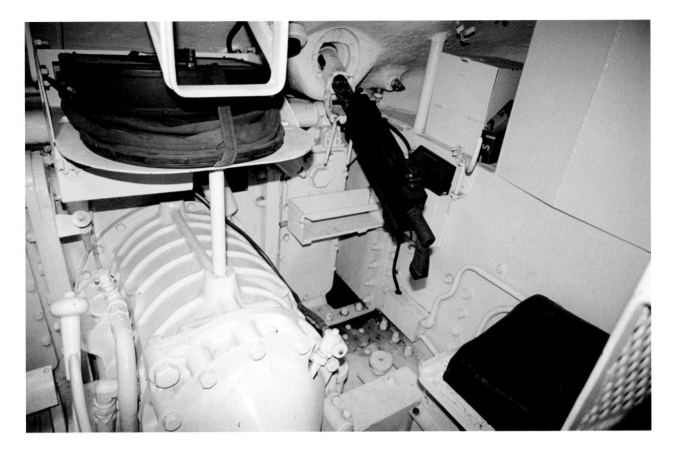

Looking forward from the loader's position on an M4A1 tank, the assistant driver's position is visible in this picture. Located just in front of the assistant driver's seat is the interior mount for a .30-caliber M1919A4 machine gun. On his left is the vehicle's transmission. *Michael Green*

came with an electrically operated windshield wiper and defroster. Power to operate them came from plugging the hood extension cable into the utility outlet socket on the driver's instrument panel. Jim Francis, an M4 series tanker with the 12th Armored Division in Europe, does not remember ever seeing a tank with the hatch hood and could never figure out why.

HULL VISION DEVICES

In early M4 series production tanks, the driver and assistant driver had emergency direct vision slots protected by armored flaps. Due to production tolerances, which resulted in very small gaps between the hull and the direct-vision armored flaps hinges, firing tests demonstrated that bullet splash could enter the front hull compartment and cause serious injury to the driver and assistant driver.

To overcome the bullet splash problem, the Ordnance Department originally decided to weld 3/8-inch

steel armored plates to the inside of the hull—around the handles used for opening the armored flaps that covered the direct-vision slots. However, with a subsequent 2-inch-long increase of the driver and assistant driver's hatch periscope mounts, it proved almost impossible for them to make use of the direct-vision slots.

The Ordnance Department then took the next logical step and dropped the direct-vision slots from the M4 series design. In their place appeared a set of fixed overhead auxiliary periscopes directly in front of the hatch periscopes. Their inclusion also eliminated the ballistics weak spot presented by the direct-vision slots in the tank's front hull.

GETTING STARTED

The driver's instrument panel was located on the left side of the driver's station. To start the tank (except for radial-engine powered vehicles), one of the turret crew members opened a fuel valve on the firewall to select the

A close-up view of the instrument panel of an early M4 series tank and the accompanying listing of its details originate from an army manual. The starter switch and the fuel cutoff switch are both marked on the instrument panel. At the top center of the panel is the four-position rotary ignition switch.

A—RIGHT-HAND UTILITY OUTLET CIRCUIT BREAKER
B—LEFT-HAND UTILITY OUTLET CIRCUIT BREAKER
C—BLACKOUT DRIVE SWITCH CIRCUIT BREAKER
D—FUEL CUT-OFF SWITCH
E—UTILITY OUTLET
F—IGNITION SWITCH
G—PRIMER PUMP
H—UTILITY OUTLET
J—BLACKOUT DRIVING LIGHT SWITCH
K—STARTER SWITCH
L—MAIN LIGHT SWITCH
M—TACHOMETER
N—TRANSMISSION OIL TEMPERATURE GAGE
P—OIL LEVEL GAGE

Q—OIL PRESSURE GAGE
R—AMMETER
S—LOW OIL PRESSURE WARNING LIGHT
T—SPEEDOMETER
U—WATER HIGH TEMPERATURE WARNING LIGHT
V—VOLTMETER (NOT USED)
W—ENGINE WATER TEMPERATURE GAGE
X—FUEL GAGE
Y—FUEL TANK SELECTOR SWITCH
Z—PANEL LIGHT RHEOSTAT SWITCH
AA—BLACKOUT DRIVE LIGHT SWITCH CIRCUIT BREAKER
BB—INSTRUMENT PANEL CIRCUIT BREAKER
CC—HORN CIRCUIT BREAKER

desired fuel tank from which to draw fuel. The driver could see how much fuel was in each tank by selecting a switch on the instrument panel and reading the level on the one fuel tank. He then turned the battery master switch to the "on" position. (The radio master switch did not go on until after the engine had started; this avoided electrical surges in the radios.) After that, he checked that the gear lever was in neutral and that the brakes were applied. He then held the clutch pedal down, or locked out the clutches. Following that, he tested the operation of the engine emergency shut-down valves and set the hand throttle to the idling position.

As a last step to starting the tank, the driver pushed the starter button and held it down firmly until the engine turned over. He checked the tachometer to make sure the engine(s) was at idle speed and checked the oil pressure gauge to ensure that the lubrication system was working. Finally, he set the hand throttle to warming-up speed and slowly engaged the clutches to allow the transmission lubricant to rise to operating temperature.

The starting procedure for radial-engine powered M4 series tanks was a bit more complex. Jacques Little-field, president of the Military Vehicle Technology Foundation, describes what it takes to get an M4 or M4A1

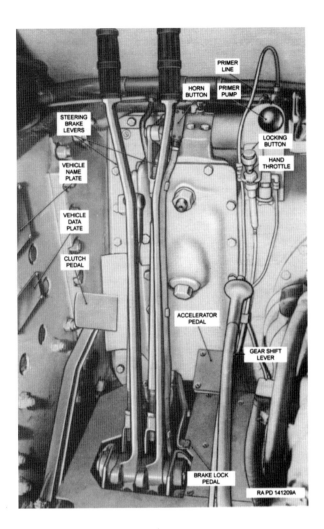

Labels (left image, top to bottom): PRIMER LINE, HORN BUTTON, PRIMER PUMP, STEERING BRAKE LEVERS, LOCKING BUTTON, HAND THROTTLE, VEHICLE NAME PLATE, VEHICLE DATA PLATE, CLUTCH PEDAL, ACCELERATOR PEDAL, GEAR SHIFT LEVER, BRAKE LOCK PEDAL, RA PD 141209A

From a U.S. Army manual is this close-up illustration of the driver's controls on an M4 series tank. The accelerator pedal regulates the engine's rpm. In conjunction with the accelerator pedal, there is a hand throttle. Just above the hand throttle is an engine primer pump to assist the driver in cold-weather starting.

with a radial engine going: "On any radial-engine vehicle, before you can start it, you have to turn the engine, making sure its magnetos are off. You put a large hand crank into a reduction gear in the back and you then have to turn the engine through about three turns. Now to get three turns through the starter, the driver has to turn about 60 or 70 times on a hand crank located at the rear of the tank. This feature proved to be very unpopular with American tankers as one could expect."

On the floor directly ahead of the driver's seat and to the right of the steering brake levers was an accelerator pedal. A hand-operated throttle sat on the final drive

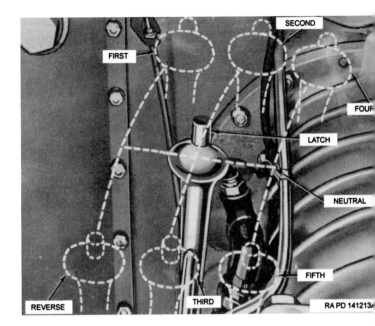

Labels (right image): SECOND, FIRST, FOUR[TH], LATCH, NEUTRAL, FIFTH, REVERSE, THIRD, RA PD 141213[A]

The gearshift lever of an M4 series tank had five forward speeds and one reverse position, as shown in this army manual illustration. On top of the gearshift level was a small knob (known as the lever latch), which prevented the driver from shifting into first gear or reverse. The driver depressed the lever latch to shift into either first gear or reverse.

housing, to the right of the steering brake levers, and just above the foot throttle. There was a lock button located in the center of the hand throttle button, which held it at the desired setting. On the left side of the steering brake levers was a floor-mounted clutch pedal. To permit shifting of gears, the driver disengaged the clutch by depressing the clutch pedal.

The gearshift lever on the M4 series was located to the right of the driver. There were five forward gears and one reverse gear. First gear was an extremely low ratio, intended to provide unusually high tractive effort, or for slow movement in restricted areas without having to slip the clutch. Normal operation used only the top four gear ratios. The driver had to depress a plunger on top of the shift lever before he could move the lever over to the left for engaging first or reverse gear. When changing into a gear, the driver moved the shift lever until he felt a resistance. He then maintained a firm pressure on the shift lever until it moved into position easily.

The M4 series driver had two steering brake levers mounted on the floor of the vehicle just forward of his

Visible on this early production M4A1 are the driver's and assistant driver's direct-view armored visors. In both their open and closed positions, the armored visors failed to keep out bullet splash and soon disappeared from the vehicle's design. *Patton Museum*

seat. The right and left steering brake levers operated the right and left brakes, respectively. The controls were not interconnected, thus operation of one steering brake lever would have no effect on the other. Braking came about by simultaneously pulling both levers. There was no separate service brake control.

For the driver to shift gears while braking on a downhill slope, he had to hold both levers back with his left hand, move the transmission lever with his right hand, and manipulate the clutch with his left foot while simultaneously controlling engine speed with his right foot. This operation left no free appendages with which the driver could brace himself, so drivers quickly learned to plan ahead to avoid such situations.

THE FINE POINTS OF DRIVING THE M4 SERIES TANKS

Steering was accomplished by pulling the appropriate steering brake lever straight back with a smooth, deliberate movement. When released, the steering brake levers always returned to their forward position. When the vehicle was moving forward, pulling back on the right steering brake lever would turn the tank to the right, while the converse would happen with the left steering brake lever. If the driver pulled hard on a steering brake

A backup vision device was provided for the driver and assistant driver of the M4 series after the elimination of the direct-view armored visors. The Ordnance Department came up with an overhead periscope located directly in front of their respective hatches, as seen in this photograph. The one pictured is in the closed position. *Michael Green*

To provide the crews of M4 series tanks some manner of exiting their vehicle other than the overhead hatches in the hull and turret, there was an escape hatch located in the hull floor behind the assistant driver's position. This posed picture shows a crew member exiting the escape hatch with his pistol drawn. *Patton Museum*

lever at high speed, he could put the vehicle into a broadside skid. The differential—whose job was to divide power between the two tracks—automatically channeled available power to the un-braked outside track that was needed to complete the turn.

Drivers applied the brakes intermittently to avoid overheating. The brakes operated in cooling oil, and the heat generated by a slipping brake could glaze the brake linings and make the brakes less effective.

The U.S. Army manuals on driving the M4 series stress that the drivers should always anticipate each turn and remain ready to apply more power as needed to compensate for the drag of a turn. Although engine power was redirected to the unbraked side, the tank required more power in a turn to compensate for the sideways slip of the tracks as the vehicle changed direction. The manual also points out that the driver's hands should be free of the steering brake levers when not actually steering the tank. Jim Francis recalls that the driver on his M4 series tank never took his hands off the steering levers, just as a car driver keeps his hands on the steering wheel for any sudden emergency.

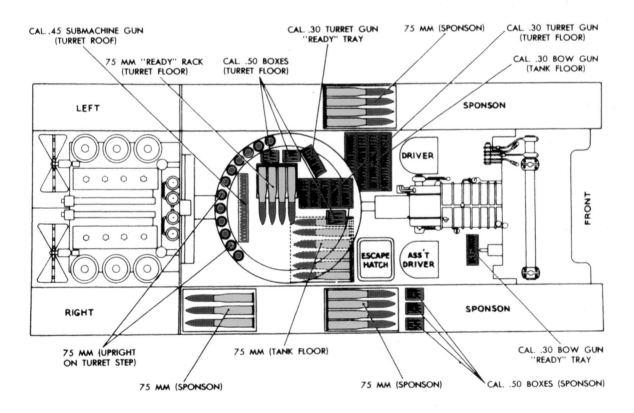

This overhead line drawing of an M4A2 tank shows the location of the main gun rounds in the vehicle as well as the small arms ammunition. The .50-caliber machine gun ammunition storage is in purple, the .30-caliber machine gun in red, and the .45-caliber submachine gun ammunition in blue. *James D. Brown*

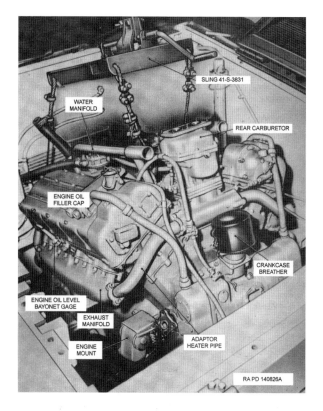

This army manual image shows a Ford GAA engine going into the rear hull of an M4A3 tank. A liquid-cooled eight-cylinder gasoline powered engine, it produced 500 net horsepower at 2,600 rpm. The engine weighed 1,470 pounds without accessories. The cylinder block and crankcase were made of cast aluminum, with steel dry-type sleeves in the cylinder bores.

If the M4 series tank was moving in a straight line on level terrain, the driver normally started out in second gear and then shifted through third and fourth, much as a car driver would with a stick-shift car. First gear was used only for maneuvering the tank in tight spaces or when driving over obstacles.

The one thing an M4 series driver never wanted to do was crash a gear by using excessive force on the gear lever. This resulted in a serious strain on the vehicle's control linkage and transmission. Therefore, even though the transmission featured gear synchronizers to allow smooth gear changes, most drivers learned to shift using the double-clutch technique borrowed from truck drivers.

To slow down or stop the M4 series tank, the driver pulled both steering levers back with equal force, or else the tank would steer to one side. Stopping the tank involved depressing the clutch pedal when the vehicle had slowed down to approximately 2 to 5 miles per hour. Once stopped, the driver set the hand throttle for a tachometer reading of 500 rpm for the duration of the halt.

To place the M4 series tank in reverse, the vehicle had to be at a standstill. With engines idling, the driver held down the clutch pedal, depressed the safety button on the gearshift lever, and moved the lever to the reverse position. In reverse, the speed of the M4 series was not supposed to exceed 3 miles per hour, with the engine rpm speed not to exceed 1,800. To steer in reverse, the driver worked the steering levers in the same way as when he drove the vehicle forward. Steering while in reverse was actually easier than in a vehicle with a steering wheel, because the driver did not need to mentally reverse his actions; whether going in forward or in reverse he always applied the brake on the track he wanted to retard.

EMERGENCY ESCAPE HATCH

The hull emergency escape hatch was located behind the assistant driver's seat and was secured by four latches, which were all connected to a single control lever for quick release. In combat, tank crews leaving a disabled

Pictured in the left-rear corner of an M4A1 tank hull is the auxiliary generator and engine that form one integral unit. Nicknamed the "Little Joe," it operated when the tank's batteries were charging or when the tank's main engine was not running. It also saw use when the current provided by the main engine proved inadequate for an imposed load. *Michael Green*

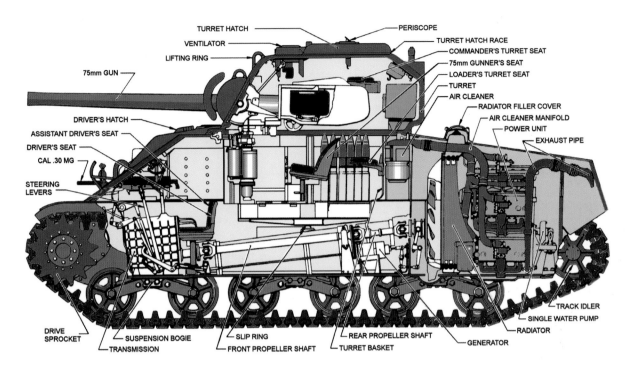

TURRET HATCH · PERISCOPE · VENTILATOR · LIFTING RING · 75mm GUN · DRIVER'S HATCH · ASSISTANT DRIVER'S SEAT · DRIVER'S SEAT · CAL .30 MG · STEERING LEVERS · DRIVE SPROCKET · SUSPENSION BOGIE · TRANSMISSION · SLIP RING · FRONT PROPELLER SHAFT · REAR PROPELLER SHAFT · TURRET BASKET · GENERATOR · TURRET HATCH RACE · COMMANDER'S TURRET SEAT · 75mm GUNNER'S SEAT · LOADER'S TURRET SEAT · TURRET · AIR CLEANER · RADIATOR FILLER COVER · AIR CLEANER MANIFOLD · POWER UNIT · EXHAUST PIPE · TRACK IDLER · SINGLE WATER PUMP · RADIATOR

This cutaway line drawing of an M4A4 tank shows the many internal and external components that make up the vehicle. The vertically stored 75mm main-gun rounds along the turret ring disappeared from later production units, as they proved very vulnerable in combat when a projectile penetrated the tank. *James D. Brown*

vehicle are fair game for all on the battlefield. Normally, machine-gun fire from opposing tanks or infantry is the preferred way in which to kill tank crews as they try to leave their vehicles.

The M4 series emergency escape hatch was also used on numerous occasions to pick up wounded soldiers. In the book *Tanks are Mighty Fine Things* appears this story by Marine Corps Private First Class Frank Upton, who was fighting the Japanese on Tinian Island in 1944:

I love tanks and everybody connected with them. When I was hit in Tinian we were on patrol and the Nips had pinned us down in a field of sugar cane. They were in caves in the cliffs and while we could see exactly nothing of them, they were really giving us the business. A machine gun slug went through my hip early and I had visions of being in the field until dark when one of those Chrysler jobs [M4 series] rolled up. The driver told me what he was going to do and after I had crawled out on harder ground, he drove the tank over me and pulled me through the escape hatch in the belly of

the tank. Those treads looked plenty big as they straddled me, but we drove back to the lines slick as a whistle.

MORE HULL DETAILS

Like most World War II tanks, the powerplant of the M4 series resided in the rear of the hull in a compartment separated from the crew compartment (also known as the fighting compartment) by a bulkhead. In the case of the M4A3 tank, the engine sat on four engine mounts: The two in the front attached to the engine compartment bulkhead and the two in the rear sat on the engine compartment floor. Between the hull floor and the engine mounts were rubber bushings to control engine vibration.

A U.S. Army manual gives this description of the rear hull arrangement on the M4 and M4A1 tanks:

Access to the engine is provided through a hinged engine compartment top plate, the rear engine doors, and the inspection plate located beneath the engine. Horizontal mufflers, running from front to rear under the engine compartment

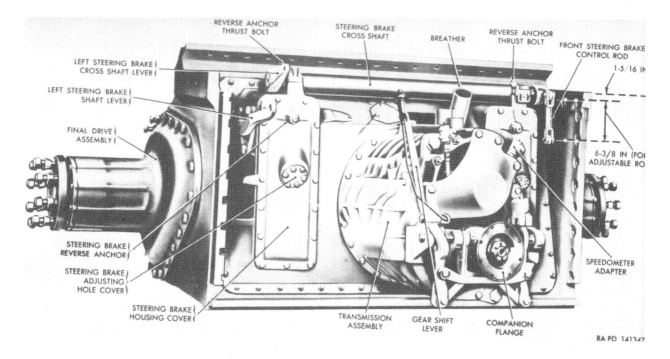

REVERSE ANCHOR
THRUST BOLT

STEERING BRAKE
CROSS SHAFT

BREATHER

REVERSE ANCHOR
THRUST BOLT

FRONT STEERING BRAKE
CONTROL ROD

LEFT STEERING BRAKE
CROSS SHAFT LEVER

LEFT STEERING BRAKE
SHAFT LEVER

FINAL DRIVE
ASSEMBLY

STEERING BRAKE
REVERSE ANCHOR

STEERING BRAKE
ADJUSTING
HOLE COVER

STEERING BRAKE
HOUSING COVER

TRANSMISSION
ASSEMBLY

GEAR SHIFT
LEVER

COMPANION
FLANGE

SPEEDOMETER
ADAPTER

1-5/16 IN

6-3/8 IN (FOI
ADJUSTABLE RO

RA PD 141347

This labeled picture of the power train assembly of an M4 series tank comes from an army manual. The power train assembly consists of the transmission, the controlled differential with steering brakes, and the final drives to which the track driving sprockets attach. The track driving sprockets do not appear in this picture.

top plates, reduce engine noise considerably below that of previous model medium tanks. The air cleaners are mounted at the rear and outside the engine compartment for easier servicing. An air inlet cover in the front engine compartment top plate gives access to the fan compartment. The tank has four fuel tanks, two vertical tanks, and two large sponson tanks, located at the right and left front of the engine compartment. They are filled through four caps located on the top of the hull to the right and left rear of the turret.

All M4 series tanks came with an engine fire extinguisher system, which consisted of two fixed 10-pound bottles of carbon dioxide clamped to the vehicle's bulkhead at the left of the fighting compartment. The extinguishers connected to six discharge nozzles through metal tubing in the engine compartment. In case of fire, the crew actuated the system manually from either inside or outside the tank, which then squirted carbon dioxide into the vehicle's engine compartment. Two portable extinguishers were also part of the tank's fire extinguisher system. One was located in the vehicle's turret and the other near the driver in the front hull.

The M4 series came with two 12-volt storage batteries located under the turret basket. Connected in series, they provided 24-volt current via the battery master switch. A separate connection to one of the two batteries supplied either a 12-volt or 24-volt current, depending on the voltage required by the installed radio equipment.

All wiring in the M4 series tanks ran through conduits both to protect the wiring and help minimize radio interference. Electrical current to the tank's turret went through a collector ring, located just below the turret subfloor. Terminal and control boxes connected the various circuits throughout the tank.

DIFFERENTIAL, TRANSMISSION, AND FINAL DRIVE DETAILS

The front lower nose of the M4 series tank hull consisted of a cast armor differential housing, which contained the tank's powertrain assembly. It bolted to the lower front hull of the tank and consisted of the controlled differential, brakes, and the final drives to which the track sprockets attached.

The design of the differential housing on early production M4 series tanks consisted of a three-piece design that bolted together. The resulting subassembly bolted to

STEERING BRAKES

This picture shows the rear of an M4 series tank differential—minus the transmission—that provides the means of steering and stopping the vehicle. The differential also allows the tank's outer track to travel faster than the inner track during turns. Clearly visible on either side of the differential gears are the large steering brakes' shoes. *Michael Green*

the lower front hull of the vehicle. An improved single-piece differential housing following the contours of the original three-piece arrangement soon appeared. This new design greatly simplified the task of removing or installing the differential housing.

A third style of differential housing appeared on the last production units of the M4 series. While still one piece, it came with a much thicker and sharper nose contour to improve the ballistic protection levels on the tank. The assembly line workers of the Detroit Tank Arsenal nicknamed this final version the "Mary Ann," because it shared a similar profile of a very statuesque young woman who also worked at the factory.

The five-speed synchromesh transmission attached to the rear of the differential housing and occupied the

front center of the hull. It incorporated a pressure-feed lubrication system in which a pump—driven from a transmission power takeoff—forced oil to the output shaft pinion bearings by way of an oil cooler, which was located in the fighting compartment bulkhead above the driveshaft housing. The speedometer was driven from the gearbox output shaft at the rear of the transmission.

The M4 series tanks used a controlled differential. The motion of the differential gears, which divided power between the two output shafts, could be controlled by the steering levers that applied brakes to one side or the other for turning. Earlier systems required disengaging the inside track from its driveshaft, which resulted in imprecise steering and added the possibility of stalling the engine as the track was re-engaged. With

An **M4A1** tank, belonging to the collection of the Military Vehicle Technology Foundation, poses for a picture. It features the original bolted three-piece cast-armored differential cover, which protects the powertrain assembly and formed the front lower portion of the tank's hull. *Michael Green*

controlled differential arrangement, both tracks drove when steering. The first country to employ a controlled differential in its tanks was France in 1926.

A disadvantage of the M4 series system was that its heavy-duty truck-type differential made it impossible to make a pivot turn (very useful in tank combat). A pivot turn is performed when one track turns forward and the other turns in reverse, thus pivoting the tank about its own turn axis. The nonboosted brakes made it physically difficult for all but the strongest drivers to make even a complete skid turn (pivoting the tank about an axis beneath a locked inside track), unless the terrain he was turning on was smooth and slippery (such as ice). The M4 series tank's normal minimum turn radius was about 80 feet.

There were many disadvantages of having the M4 series differential, final drive casing, and transmission in

the lower front hull. It forced the tank's designers to make the vehicle taller than desirable, because they had to allow extra room for the driveshaft to pass under the vehicle's turret to transfer power to the front-mounted transmission. Front-mounted transmissions and differentials were more vulnerable to antitank mines because most mines would go off under the front sections of vehicles.

The main advantage of having the M4 series differential, final drive casing, and transmission in the lower front hull was the added level of protection it afforded the crew by absorbing incoming armor-piercing (AP) projectiles or shaped charge warheads.

SUSPENSION SYSTEM

In the 1930s, the Ordnance Department had developed a number of high-speed light tanks, with their hulls supported by a coil spring suspension unit mounted on

This photograph of an M4A1 tank shows the one-piece differential armored cover featuring the same contours as the original bolted three-piece armored transmission cover. The one-piece design made it much easier to install and service both the differential and the final drives. *Patton Museum*

The final design for the one-piece differential-armored cover on M4 series tanks featured a much thicker sharp-nosed contour to improve the vehicle's ballistic protection, as seen in this picture of an M4 composite hull tank. This particular armored cover design was nicknamed the "Mary Ann" by the workers at the Detroit Tank Arsenal, in honor of a shapely female coworker. *Patton Museum*

German antitank mines posed a serious threat to M4 series tanks, as is evident in a photograph showing an M4A3 that ran over two 21-pound Teller mines. Like most antitank mines, the fuses on these required more pressure than would be exerted by a walking infantryman, thus ensuring the mine would only detonate under a vehicle. *Patton Museum*

axles. Two small metal wheels, known as bogie wheels, were mounted at the ends of each axle. This basic system, referred to as the vertical volute suspension system (VVSS), was adapted by lengthening the M3 series tank in 1940 and the M4 series in 1941.

The VVSS takes its name from the volute springs, which are helically wound steel strips whose inner turns are displaced along the central axis to give the finished spring a conical shape. Unlike a torsion spring (commonly found in watches), which takes its load by applying reaction torque around its central axis, the volute spring takes compression loads along its axis. Volute springs are compact and have the advantage, in tank applications, of being damage tolerant. Unlike helical springs, coil springs, or torsion bars, if a portion of the volute spring is damaged, the broken pieces can carry at least part of the original load.

The early M4 series production tanks featured a track return roller that sat on top of the bogie-carrying bracket, while later production vehicles of the M4 series had the track return roller mounted behind the bogie-carrying bracket.

This extract from an M4A3 army manual details how the VVSS suspension functioned:

The vehicle is supported on six suspension assemblies [three on each side of the tank's hull]. Each suspension assembly consists of two rubber-tired suspension wheels, two volute [coil] springs, a volute suspension bracket that houses the volute springs, track skid, and a track support roller. As the vehicle passes over uneven ground, the vertical movement of the suspension [bogie] wheels is transferred to the supporting arms or levers and is absorbed by the two volute springs in each suspension assembly. Two drive sprockets at the front of the vehicle pull the tracks from the rear and lay them down in front of the advancing suspension assemblies. A track skid and a track support roller are mounted at the top of each suspension assembly, to support and carry the upper portion of the track. An adjustable idler wheel for each track is mounted at the rear of the vehicle for adjusting and retaining the tension of the track.

TANK TRACK PROBLEMS

In World War I, tank tracks consisted of heavy continuous articulated bands of steel links (also known as shoes) connected by steel pins. The pins and links wore out

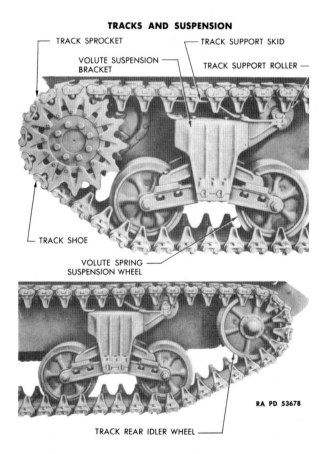

TRACKS AND SUSPENSION

TRACK SPROCKET
TRACK SUPPORT SKID
VOLUTE SUSPENSION BRACKET
TRACK SUPPORT ROLLER
TRACK SHOE
VOLUTE SPRING SUSPENSION WHEEL
RA PD 53678
TRACK REAR IDLER WHEEL

This photograph from an U.S. Army manual has labeled the various components that make up the vertical volute spring suspension (VVSS) system on the M4 series tank. Each of the drive sprocket assembly consists of two sprockets bolted to a hub. The hub bolts to the flanged end of the tank's final driveshaft.

rapidly, and failures due to broken tracks were frequent. With the advent of higher-speed light tanks in the 1930s, the Ordnance Department developed a track system made up of smooth rubber track blocks (also known as pads) molded onto a steel framework.

When the need arose for off-road operations, tank crews could bolt detachable steel grousers to some of the rubber blocks for better traction. However the tanks tended to encounter so many different types of terrain, so it proved impractical to attach and remove the grousers at every turn. To solve this problem, the Ordnance Department began putting a chevron (V-shaped) pattern on the outside of each track block in 1941. It solved many of the traction problems encountered when tanks went off-road. However, just as its development finished in early 1942, a rubber shortage forced the Ordnance Department to look for a substitute.

The rubber crisis, beginning in December 1941, was due to the Japanese seizure of the Southeast Asian countries that produced the world's rubber supply. The Under Secretary of War directed the Ordnance Department to cease production of rubber-block track at the earliest possible date, as a sufficient supply of synthetic rubber was unavailable, and begin development of all steel tracks.

By June 1942, the chief of the Ordnance Department reported that work on the development of steel track had progressed to the point that it would be possible to switch over by the end of the year. However, by March 1943, nothing had happened.

Thereafter began an almost comical series of orders and counterorders regarding the rubber-block tracks versus steel tracks. Due to the very successful showing of rubber-block tracks during the fighting in North Africa in early 1943, the Ordnance Department recommended that developmental work on all steel tracks cease in favor of rubber-block track. One of the AGF senior officers concurred with the Ordnance Department and ordered all tanks going overseas have only rubber-block tracks.

At this same time, the U.S. Army Service Forces (ASF) ordered the Ordnance Department to put only the newly developed steel tracks on tanks used for training in the United States. No sooner did this occur when the Armored Force informed the ASF that the new steel tracks were tearing up paved roads. The ASF promptly acceded to the Armored Force request and ordered the Ordnance Department to end steel track production and place only rubber-block tracks on all tanks in the United States or going overseas.

An American soldier examines a groove carved out of the armor on the lower front hull of a disabled M4 tank by a German AP projectile. Another AP projectile achieved a hull penetration in the right sponson (see arrow). The tracks on this tank were fitted with extended end connectors (nicknamed duckbills or duck feet) on the outside for better flotation over soft ground. *Patton Museum*

Taking the principle of extended end connectors one step further, the Ordnance Department had Chrysler Corporation design 4 1/2-inch spacers, which fitted in between a tank's hull and its VVSS system. This provided enough room to mount extended end connectors on both the inside and outside of M4 series tanks tracks, as shown in this photograph of an M4A3E9 tank. *Patton Museum*

The ultimate in M4 series tank track flotation devices turned out to be the 32 1/2-inch grousers (nicknamed "platypus"), which bolted to extended end connectors already fitted on the outside of a tank's tracks for a total width of 37 inches. This was enough to bring the tank's ground pressure to 7 psi. *Patton Museum*

In mid-1943, the tankers operating in Sicily (July to August 1943) and Italy (beginning in September 1943) informed all concerned that the rubber-block tracks were falling apart in less than 500 miles of use and requested the more durable steel tracks. Just before relating this information, the same tankers had requested the production of chevron tracks made of natural rubber, despite the fact that America's stockpile of the material was running low, because they found them superior to any other type of track. (Modern tracked vehicles have used steel links with replaceable rubber pads for decades.)

In view of this situation, the ASF authorized the Ordnance Department to ship steel tracks from existing stocks to oversea commanders when requested. It then told the Ordnance Department to resume steel track production.

In the early part of 1943, the American rubber industry managed to successfully coat a track block with synthetic rubber, but could not make one with an acceptable

rubber chevron. In August 1943, the AGF authorized the Ordnance Department to start the production of the synthetic rubber tracks, but also to work with industry on overcoming any problems in the development of a rubber chevron, which it eventually did.

In the meantime, the American rubber industry came up with rubber-backed steel tracks that overcame the many drawbacks of all steel tracks, such as more difficult steering and greater wear on bogie wheels. New steel track production in 1944 consisted mainly of this improved type.

The frustrations of all concerned regarding what type of track to build is related in this passage from the army official history of World War II: "In December 1943 ASF headquarters, recognizing the futility of overall directives prescribing the type of tank track to be issued, granted the Chief of Ordnance authority to manufacture both steel and rubber tracks and to issue whatever type he and the

This illustration from an army manual shows the various components of an M4 series turret. Directly below the turret is the recessed ball bearing turret race assembly (also known as the turret ring) on which the turret rotates. The turret basket bolts to the turret race ring and rotates in conjunction with the turret.

using arms jointly determined to be the most suitable for specific operations."

Early steel tracks used on U.S. Army tanks had shallow cleats, or exterior integral steel grousers, to provide traction on slippery surfaces. Deeper cleats appeared on the steel tracks toward the middle of World War II, as American tanks had to travel through deep mud and swamps more often. The designs employed for the exterior of the integral grousers included a number of different patterns; however, the Armored Force generally preferred the chevron design, which was not unlike the tread design pattern developed for the original rubber-block tracks.

A U.S. Army observer—who spoke with many of those who took part in the American military invasion

of the Japanese-occupied island of Okinawa in April to May 1945—wrote this with regard to M4 series tracks: "The only major deficiency in the medium tank was the excessive ground pressure, which prevented the medium tank from negotiating the soft terrain. The smooth rubber track has no traction, the steel track was too heavy, and in mud, the rubber chevron track was little more effective than the smooth rubber track. The best performing track was the smooth rubber track with grousers on every other block."

INCREASING TANK TRACK FLOTATION

A tank's mobility is a product of several factors. One of these factors is ground pressure, a ratio of the tank's weight to the surface area supporting this weight on the ground. In the vernacular of the time, ground pressure was usually referred to as flotation. This term does not imply ability to float in water, but the perceived ability of a tank to "float" over soft terrain.

When fitted with extended end connectors (nicknamed duckbills or duck feet), the first-generation M4 series tracks, which were 16.5 inches wide, could be increased to 20 1/8 inches wide. This increased the tank's flotation by 21 percent, and for vehicles weighing 35 tons or less, it brought the ground pressure to less than 12 psi. Although what the AGF actually wanted was to bring the ground pressure down to 7 psi, accomplishing this would have extended the tracks to an overall width for a tank in excess of 124 inches. (The standard M4 series tank was 103 inches wide.) That would have been in violation of the maximum shipping width permitted at the time.

In October 1944, the ASF ordered that all M4 series tanks shipped overseas be capable of mounting the extended end connectors. Some M4 series tanks had their suspension systems spaced out from the vehicle's hull, allowing for the use of extended end connectors on both sides of the tracks and giving an effective track width of almost 24 inches.

Another late-war effort at increasing the flotation of M4 series tanks is described in this extract from the official U.S. Army history of World War II:

A further application of the extension principle was approved in January 1945. It was an extended grouser, nicknamed the platypus, that could be bolted to extended end connectors to improve both flotation and traction. The term grouser was used to describe either detachable cleats, which could be

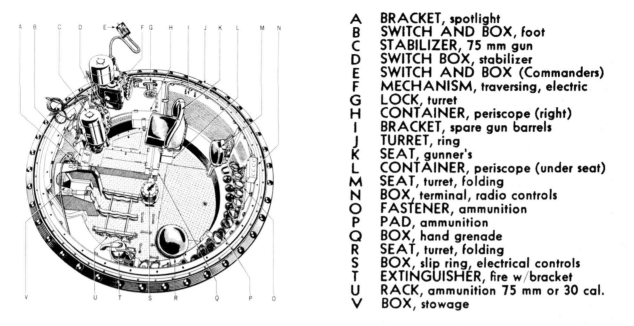

A	BRACKET, spotlight
B	SWITCH AND BOX, foot
C	STABILIZER, 75 mm gun
D	SWITCH BOX, stabilizer
E	SWITCH AND BOX (Commanders)
F	MECHANISM, traversing, electric
G	LOCK, turret
H	CONTAINER, periscope (right)
I	BRACKET, spare gun barrels
J	TURRET, ring
K	SEAT, gunner's
L	CONTAINER, periscope (under seat)
M	SEAT, turret, folding
N	BOX, terminal, radio controls
O	FASTENER, ammunition
P	PAD, ammunition
Q	BOX, hand grenade
R	SEAT, turret, folding
S	BOX, slip ring, electrical controls
T	EXTINGUISHER, fire w/bracket
U	RACK, ammunition 75 mm or 30 cal.
V	BOX, stowage

An illustration from an army M4 series tank service parts catalog shows a detailed view of all the parts and components that make up a turret basket. The arrangement is from an early production tank, as indicated by the exposed ready round racks on the turret basket floor, as well as the twelve vertical clips and base for the storage of twelve main gun rounds around the turret basket step.

fastened to the track to provide more traction, or the tread design on the track block. In the latter sense, it was termed an integral grouser. The 32.5-inch grousers, which extended from the inside of the track block outward beyond the extended end connectors, required no modification of the suspension and gave the tank a ground pressure of approximately 8 pounds per square inch. Longer grousers, 37 inches in length, were also developed for attachment to Sherman tanks equipped with spaced-out suspensions and extended end connectors on both sides of the track. The long grouser brought the ground pressure down to 7 pounds, the figure that the Army Ground Forces had earlier fixed as the optimum for effective operation. Both the long and the short grousers could be installed in the field. Both were approved for production early in 1945.

What did American tankers think about the M4 series tank's mobility compared to late-war German tanks? Lieutenant Colonel Wilson M. Hawkins of the 2nd Armored Division makes the following statement in a World War II report: "It has been claimed that our tank is the more maneuverable. In recent tests, we put a cap-

tured German Mark V [Panther] against all models of our own. The German tank was the faster, both across country and on the highway and would make sharper turns. It was also the better hill climber."

Technical Sergeant Willard D. May of the 2nd Armored Division backs up Hawkins' claim in his own interview: "I have taken instructions on the Mark V [Panther] and have found, first, it is easily as maneuverable as the Sherman; second, the flotation exceeds that of the Sherman."

Staff Sergeant Charles A. Carden, a tank platoon sergeant, completes the comparison in his report: "The Mark V [Panther] and VI [Tiger] in my opinion have more maneuverability and certainly more flotation. I have seen in many cases where the Mark V and VI tanks could maneuver nicely over ground where the M4 would bog down. On one occasion I saw at least 10 Royal Tigers [Tiger B] make a counterattack against us over ground that for us was nearly impassable."

TURRET

The one-piece cast turret atop the M4 could be traversed 360 degrees in either direction. It rotated on a recessed circular ball bearing race either manually or with an

This picture shows the turret of an M4 series tank, with the tank commander's overhead rotating split hatch clearly visible. The lack of an overhead hatch for the loader (referred to in the army manual as a door) identifies this as an early production model. Visible just in front of the commander hatch is the gunner's periscope in the closed position. The armored cover for the turret ventilator is at center. *Jim Mesko*

electro-hydraulic or an electrical power traversing system. The latter system received power from a 220 DC turret motor generator set.

Electro-hydraulic means the hydraulic system is energized by an electrically driven pump, rather than being shaft-driven. This meant that turret power was available when the tank's main engine was not running. Electricity came from the batteries or from an auxiliary generator, nicknamed the "Little Joe," which was driven by a single cylinder, two-stroke, air-cooled gasoline engine. The Little Joe sat in the left rear of the fighting compartment and was accessible by the three men in the turret.

A turret ring, located in the hull roof of a tank, is the circular opening in which the turret bearing fits. The size of the main gun and its ammunition dictates the minimum diameter of a tank's turret ring. It must be of sufficient size to allow the crew both to elevate and depress the main gun while still being able to load it. The M4 series armed with a 75mm main gun featured a turret ring of 69 inches. In comparison, the U.S. Army's M1 series of main battle tanks, armed with a 120mm main gun, featured a turret ring width of 85.5 inches.

Beneath the visible part of the M4 series turret was the turret basket or platform. It rotated with the turret and formed a floor for the turret crew to stand on. It attached to the turret by a ring of bolts around its top circumference. For safety reasons, the turret basket came encased in metal screening, but this was often removed by the crews for accessibility to the various parts of the hull.

The turret crew (also known as the gun crew) for the M4 series consisted of three men: the tank commander, gunner, and loader. The tank commander had two padded seats; the lower seat attached to a turret ring mount located on the right of the 75mm main gun and just above one of the vehicle's portable fire extinguishers.

An American soldier points to the hole in the side of an M4 series tank turret, no doubt from a large German antitank projectile. To the right of the turret penetration is a closed pistol port. While typically used to load main gun ammunition rounds into the tank's turret when open, it also proved useful as a bodily waste disposal exit. A second projectile hit just above the pistol port, penetrating and blowing off the loader's hatch. *Patton Museum*

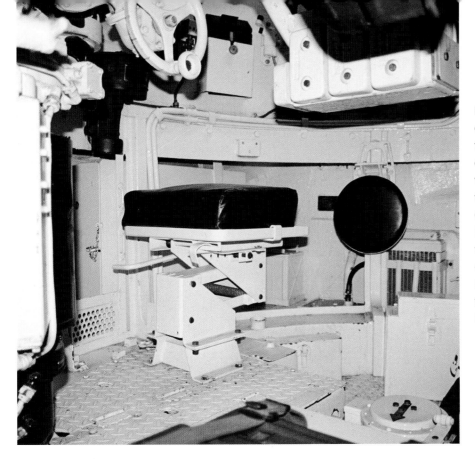

Looking into the turret from the driver's position on an M4 series tank, the gunner's seat (mounted on the turret basket floor) is visible without its backrest. Also the tank commander's lower seat (circular black pad) is seen here in its stowed vertical position. It was from this position that he often stood with his head and upper torso projecting out over the top of his overhead hatch. *Michael Green*

The seat folded out of the way when not in use. To maximize height, the tank commander could sit on an upper seat that was attached to the turret wall and also folded out of the way when not in use.

Just above the vehicle commander's two seats, in the roof of the M4 series tank turret, was an armored rotating split hatch. It was equipped with an antiaircraft machine gun mount and a rotating periscope with a 360-degree traverse. Also on the roof was a small spotlight that could be stored inside the vehicle when not required.

Just below and in front of the tank commander's position was the gunner's position. His padded seat, with a detachable padded backrest, attached to the bottom of the turret basket floor. The loader's position was on the left side of the 75mm main gun. His adjustable pad seat attached to the tank's turret ring and folded upward when not in use. There was a single electrically powered ventilating blower located in the turret roof, along with three dome lights.

The loader and gunner entered and left the vehicle through the tank commander's overhead hatch. In peacetime, this was not a problem. In combat, however, it was a different story because the M4 series burned so easily and so fast when hit by various weapons. Many loaders suffered horrible deaths because of their inability to leave the M4 series turrets in a timely manner due to the large recoil guard that bisected the inside of the turret.

A U.S. Army field service modification work order, dated September 1943, permitted the recoil guards in all M4 series tanks to be modified by the crews so that they would hinge at the rear, thus providing the loaders a better chance at survival.

The Ordnance Department soon took the next logical step and, in late 1943, ordered that all M4 series tanks be fitted with a small oval armored hatch over the loader's position. The new loader hatch first appeared on M4A1 tanks coming off the assembly lines of the Pressed Steel Car Company in November 1943. Fisher and Chrysler made the modification the following month.

Located just behind the loader position in the early production units of the M4 series turret was a 12x12-inch armored flap that opened and closed with a handle. Referred to as a pistol port (which was a misnomer), it allowed ammunition to be passed into the turret by a man standing on the ground, rather than having to first pass it up to a man standing on the hull beside the turret. This freed a crew member to perform other duties while the tank was being rearmed. It was also an easy way to eject spent main-gun cartridge cases. The other manner in which the loader could load his tank with main-gun rounds or eject spent main gun cartridge cases was through his overhead hatch. Added benefits of the pistol port were the light it allowed inside the vehicle when opened and the increased ventilation.

From the tank commander's side of the turret in an M4 series tank is this picture showing both the loader's overhead rotating periscope and the M3 smoke mortar. Fixed in elevation, it could only be aimed by pointing the tank's turret in the chosen direction. It is obvious from the photograph why U.S. Army tank loaders felt it infringed on their working space. *Michael Green*

Obviously, the pistol port in the side of the M4 series was a serious ballistic weak spot. Much discussion went on about its true value among the Ordnance Department. It all came to a head in February 1943 when a decision came to delete it from all future production M4 series tanks. Several months later, reports from the field showed that the pistol port was very necessary after all. By early 1944, it reappeared on M4 series production tanks.

All M4 series tank turrets came with a turret bustle, which was an extension on the rear of the turret and allowed room for radios and other gear inside the armor envelope. The gun could not recoil farther than the turret ring, nor could the recoil guard protrude beyond it, because it would strike the bearing at certain elevations. The bustle also counterbalanced the gun weight, making it easier to turn the turret when the vehicle was on a slope.

Due to a British request, beginning in the fall of 1943, M4 series tanks coming off the assembly lines were fitted with a British-developed smoke grenade launcher that resided in the tank's turret on the loader's side at a fixed angle. In the U.S. Army, its designation was 2-inch Mortar M3. It was not popular with American tankers, since the loaders considered it to be in the way. The Ordnance Department ordered it dropped from later production vehicles. Most surviving M4 series tanks have the hole welded over.

On the standard first-generation M4 series tank, the front of the turret was 3 inches thick, while the turret's gun shield and rotor shield together ranged between 3 and 3 1/2 inches thick, depending on the model of the tank. The roof of the turret was 1 inch thick, and the side and rear armor was 2 inches thick.

TURRET-MOUNTED MACHINE GUNS

Located on the very top of the M4 series turret was the provision for mounting a .50-caliber M2 machine gun, for operation by the tank commander. It had a barrel

A tank commander fires the M2 .50-caliber machine gun mounted on the roof of the M4 series tanks. Because firing the machine gun detracted from the tank commander's primary duties, the cupola was often rotated to the rear to allow another soldier (frequently an accompanying infantryman) to stand on the rear engine deck to fire the weapon. Also visible in this picture is the tank commander's metal vane sight used to rough aim the turret in azimuth. *Patton Museum*

length of 45 inches and weighed about 84 pounds. It could theoretically fire at 450 to 550 rounds per minute. In reality, the operator of the weapon fired in short bursts to prevent the barrel from overheating and because he could not easily observe tracers while firing the gun. Maximum effective range of the .50-caliber machine gun was a bit over 1,200 yards.

While originally intended to be an antiaircraft weapon, the turret-mounted .50-caliber machine gun saw use on almost anything that did not require the firing of the 75mm main gun. Lieutenant Colonel William Hamberg of the 5th Armored Division remembers, "The .50 caliber machine gun was constantly fired at anything that could hide a German antitank weapon of any sort. In farm country, the machine gun was always fired at large and small haystacks. If the .50 caliber ammo hit

something hard inside the haystack and bounced off, it would be immediately fired upon with the 75mm main gun. We also liked the fact that the .50 caliber machine gun could fire an incendiary round, which was excellent for setting wooden barns on fire."

Jim Francis recalls how effective the .50-caliber machine gun was against ground targets. He also remembers how ineffective it was as an aircraft gun since the operator could not move his body around enough to follow an aircraft in flight.

Author Belton Y. Cooper, in his book titled *Death Traps: The Survival of an American Armored Division in World War II*, describes the power of the .50-caliber machine gun: "The Germans had no weapon comparable to our .50 caliber . . . machine gun. If this massive slug penetrated the torso, the hydraulic shock would

On this particular M4 series tank turret, the tank commander has a .30-caliber machine gun mounted, in lieu of the normal M2 .50-caliber machine gun. In September 1942, the Ordnance Committee recommend that the M2 .50-caliber machine gun be replaced with the much smaller and lighter .30-caliber machine gun. Combat experience showed this to be a mistake and the M2 reappeared in April 1943. *Patton Museum*

generate a virtual explosion inside the body. If an arm or leg was struck, the entire limb might be severed. The Germans were terrified of it."

British and Canadian armies' tank units did not favor the mounting of the .50-caliber machine gun on the M4 series turret. More often, British Army tankers tended to use the .30-caliber machine gun on a turret mount, as did some American M4 series tankers, who would mount it in place of the .50-caliber machine gun.

Jim Carroll recalls that in his Marine Corps tank unit on Iwo Jima, his crew never even bothered to mount the .50-caliber machine gun since one would have to expose his entire body to the enemy in order to fire the weapon.

In a wartime U.S. Army publication Lieutenant Zachman, an M4 series tank platoon leader, states, "A .30-caliber machine gun on the antiaircraft mount comes in handy; it can be operated more easily than the .50 caliber and enables the tank commander to stay lower in the turret while he is firing it. The more plentiful supply of .30 caliber ammunition is an additional advantage."

In an article in the November–December 1954 issue of *Armor* magazine, titled "Tanks in Korea 1950-1953," appears this statement regarding the turret-mounted .50 caliber machine gun: "A tank commander is more effective when he fights his crew [provides overall command of the tank] than when he spends a large part of the action firing the turret-mounted cal. 50 machine gun.

The .50 cal turret gun is advantageous when tanks are giving overhead fire support to advancing infantry, not when the attack is primarily a tank action."

Located to the left of the main gun on the M4 series turret was an M1919A4 .30-caliber machine gun, referred to as the coaxial, that elevated and traversed along with the main gun. The gunner fired it with a foot-operated electrical switch. The loader was responsible for replacing the ammunition containers when its ammunition was exhausted, clearing stoppages, and changing worn barrels.

In the event of failure of the gunner's foot-operated trigger, the loader could also fire the coaxial .30-caliber machine with a trigger located on the rear face of the receiver. The coaxial machine gun saw use on anything that did not require a main gun round, such as enemy infantry or nonarmored vehicles, and was the most commonly used weapon on all M4 series tanks.

OTHER WEAPONS

For dismounted use, all M4 series tanks carried two metal tripods, one for a .30-caliber machine gun and the other for the .50-caliber machine guns. Also carried on M4 series tanks was at least one Model 1928A1 Thompson submachine guns, later replaced by the M3 submachine gun, nicknamed the "Grease Gun." The small M1 carbine appeared on some tanks, but was not a preferred weapon because its 15-round magazines were smaller than the 30-round magazines of the submachine guns and fired a less lethal round. M4 series tanks also carried at least a dozen hand grenades.

Although not talked about much, the tracks on M4 series would be used as weapons in running over and crushing enemy soldiers. On a number of occasions where dug-in enemy infantry refused to surrender, an M4 series tank track dropped into a slit trench and then "spun like crazy"—quickly taking care of the occupants. General Bruce C. Clarke, a combat commander in the 4th Armored Division and later the 7th Armored Division, says, "The track is in itself a major weapon system on the tank."

COMMUNICATION EQUIPMENT

M4 series vehicle commanders and platoon leaders could choose from a number of different communications means including messenger, wire, visual, sound, or radio. A U.S. Army manual, dated January 12, 1942, listed the bugle as an approved means of tank-to-tank communications.

One might guess that the manual's authors spent many years in the cavalry. Bugles were not normally part of the table of organization of army tank units.

The most secure means available for vehicle commanders and platoon leaders (there were five tanks in a platoon) to transmit lengthy messages was to use a messenger. Commanders used messengers who would deliver—on foot, motorcycle, or jeep—platoon fire plans and status reports to higher headquarters.

When companies (there were seventeen tanks in a company) set up their tanks in initial defensive positions, assembly areas, or other static situations, crews could lay wire from one tank to another to communicate with the platoon leader's vehicle. Crews could also connect field telephones to the wire, allowing platoon leaders to communicate with observation posts or company command posts.

Visual signals consisted of either hand-and-arm or flag signals to control individual tank and platoon movements. Each tank came with a cased set of red, green, and yellow flags. Flags served as an extension of hand-and-arm signals when the distance between vehicles became too great. Tank crew members could also use pyrotechnic ammunition (flares) to illuminate an area at night or as a signal for friendly unit identification, maneuver element control, target marking, and location reports.

The most flexible but least secure means of communication between tanks has, until recently, always been the radio. Now that today's tankers have frequency-hopping digital radios, they have become much more secure. The radio can quickly transmit information over long distances with great accuracy. However, radio signals are vulnerable to enemy interception or jamming. Tank platoons and individual tanks would normally use the radio when other means of communication proved unavailable

In the rear of U.S. Army M4 series turrets was one of three different types of frequency modulated (FM) radio sets, these being the SCR-508, SCR-528 or the SCR-68B. All of them had a top range of 10–20 miles under favorable conditions (line of sight). Under poor conditions, range could go down to under 5 miles. Power for the radios came from the vehicle's batteries through a separate wiring system.

Another radio set sometimes found on M4 series tanks was the amplitude modulated (AM) radio designated AN/VRC-3, which was the vehicular adaptation of the standard American military infantry radio

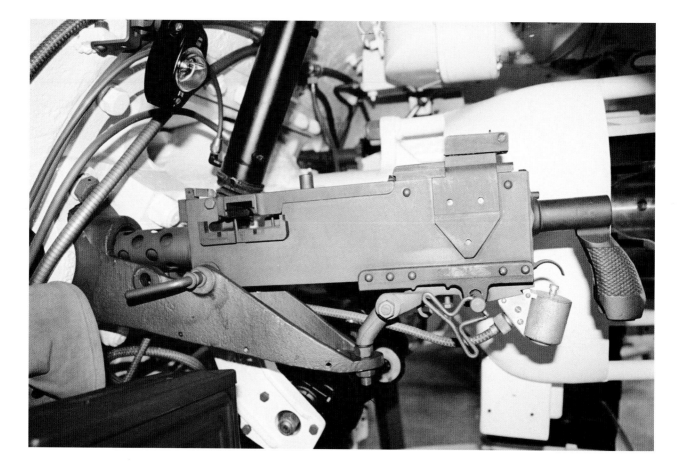

Visible in this picture is the coaxial .30-caliber machine that mounted on the left side of the 75mm main gun in the M4 series. The cylindrical electric firing solenoid is beneath the trigger. When the gunner depressed a foot switch, the plunger of the solenoid extended upward to contact the trigger. In an emergency, the loader could pull the trigger with his finger. *Michael Green*

communication set known as the walkie-talkie. (The walkie-talkie was a backpack-mounted radio, whose nickname is often confused with the handy-talkie, an early handheld unit that was held up to the ear when in use.) It provided short-range communication in combat areas between tank company commanders and tank platoon leaders or ground troops. It was secured to the left wall of the turret just forward of the loader's position.

Unlike the arrangement in modern American tanks that allow all crew members to hear and transmit, the tank commander and loader were the only crew members on the M4 series tanks that could operate the AN/VRC-3. It operated on either a battery, which was contained in a case secured to the set, or the tank's power supply.

On the right and left rear top of M4 series tank turrets were small openings for the installation of an antenna mast base. It consisted of a large flexible helical spring and a feed-through porcelain insulator at the rear of an installed FM radio set, as well as provisions on the bottom for connecting the antenna lead-in. Three mast sections, made of high-tensile-strength steel tubing screwed together, formed a whip antenna that attached to the mast base.

When an M4 series tank received the AN/VRC-3, the whip antenna mast base fitted to the left rear top of the turret bustle, or at the right front hull of welded-hull models. Tank crews typically kept antennae tied down to reduce damage from striking tree limbs or other overhead obstructions when traveling at speed, and to avoid disclosing presence of a vehicle behind cover.

CREW COMMUNICATIONS

During World War II all American tankers wore a padded composite-fiber crash helmet fastened together

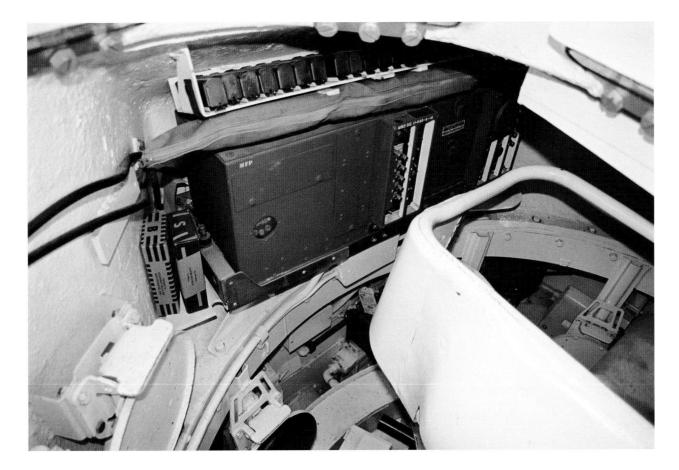

Looking almost directly down the tank commander's hatch on an M4A1 tank, one can see the tank commander's upper and lower seats, both in their stowed positions. To the right of the seats is the radio located in the rear turret bustle. On top of the radio is one of the crew's submachine guns in a zippered canvas bag. On top of the canvas bag containing the submachine gun are thirty-round magazines for the weapon. *Michael Green*

with narrow straps of leather or elastic webbing material. (Copied from prewar football helmets, many of these helmets were manufactured by the Wilson Sporting Goods Company.) Inserted within this crash helmet were earplugs or small round earphones for the crewmembers to listen to either the vehicle's intercom system (referred to as an interphone system in army wartime manuals) or the radio.

To transmit over the intercom, some M4 series tank crew members wore a throat microphone, which consisted of two small button-shaped plastic devices fastened against the larynx by a combination of an elastic band and a metal clip. When an operator wished to speak, he first needed to depress a switch on his chest set. When he did speak, his vocal chords sent up a vibration in the small button shaped transmitters, which then went out over the intercom or the radio. The advantage

of this system was that the microphones did not pick up the background noise from weapons firing or operation of the tank. Additionally, the microphones did not ice up from exhaled breath in cold weather. By the closing stages of the war, a lip microphone was used.

M4 series tank commanders had access to a handheld microphone to transmit their verbal orders rather than depending on a throat microphone. The shape of this microphone gave it the nickname of "pork chop." A spare pork chop attached to a hook behind the loader's position.

Jim Carroll recalls that in his vehicle, the tank commander did not want other members of the crew talking on the intercom, as it would interfere with the radio messages coming in. Because they stayed in one location for up to 30 minutes while providing fire support to Marine Corps infantry units, the normal means of com-

This picture of a 2nd Armored Division tanker shows the standard football-style helmet worn by M4 series tank crewmen. Under each of the two earflaps were hard plastic earpiece receivers, connected with a toggle switch on the tanker's chest. Tankers could talk to each other (or over the radio) by pressing down on the toggle switch and transmitting their voice with two small throat induction microphones or a handheld microphone. *Patton Museum*

The Marine Corps had favored light tanks going into World War II; however, combat experience demonstrated that the tanks lacked the firepower to effectively deal with well-built Japanese defensive positions. To rectify this situation the marines took into service the M4A2 tanks, with their 75mm main gun firing a very potent HE round. *Patton Museum*

munications within the tank was shouting at each other. Jim Francis also remembers that in his tank, only the tank commander had the ability to talk over the intercom, as nobody wore the throat mikes.

Because the crash helmet offered no protection from bullets or shell fragments, some M4 series crew members also wore a foam-padded set of plastic earphones (first available in 1944) that could be fitted under the standard steel helmet. Most tankers who did not have access to the foam-padded earphone sets would merely take the liner out of a large steel helmet and jam the outer steel pot over the crash helmet.

From a World War II issue of the *Marine Corps Gazette* is an example of what you might have heard between M4 series crews during combat. A U.S. Navy destroyer lying offshore during the Battle of Guam in 1944 made a recording of the radio communication between Marine Corps tanks' crew members engaged in a fight with Japanese units against a background of gunfire, mortar explosions, and engine noise. The radio chatter shows that even when radios worked well, they did not guarantee clarity of communication in a confusing battle. The following example demonstrates this point:

To defeat Japanese antitank infantry squads armed with Molotov cocktails (bottled gasoline), magnetic antitank mines, and satchel charges of explosives, marine tankers began to mount a variety of objects on the exterior of their M4 series tanks for a measure of extra protection. The crew of the M4A3 tank pictured here welded extra track links to both the hull and turret of its vehicles, as well as stacking sandbags on the front upper hull. *Patton Museum*

This is Red Two, Red One. Heartburn says that he is ready to start shooting at those pillboxes.

Tell Heartburn I can't receive him. You will have to relay. Tell him to give us a signal and we'll spot for him.

Red Two, wilco.

Heartburn, raise your fire. You're right into us.

That's not Heartburn, Red Two. That's a high-velocity gun from our left rear. I heard it whistle. Red One out.

Red Three, this is Red One. Can you see that gun that's shooting at us?

Red One, I think that's our own gunfire.

Goddammit, it's not, I tell you. It's a high-velocity gun and not a howitzer. Investigate over there on your left. But watch out for the infantry; they're right in there somewhere.

Red Two, tell Heartburn down fifty, left fifty.

Red Two, wilco.

Red Three, what are you doing? Go southwest.

I am heading southwest, Red One.

For Christ's sake, get oriented. I can see you, Red Three. You are heading northwest. Fox Love with hard left brake. Cross the road and go back up behind that house.

But!

I don't know why I bother with you, Red Three. Yellow One, take charge of Red Three and get him squared away. And get that gun; it's too close.

Red One from Red Two, Heartburn wants to know if we are the front lines.

Tell him, Christ, yes. We're plenty front right now.

This is Red Two. Artillery on the way.

Red One, wilco. . . .

Red One from Yellow One. I can see some Japs setting up a machine gun about 100 yards to my right.

Those are our troops, Yellow One. Don't shoot in there.

The man at my telephone—I think he's an officer—says we have no troops in there.

Yellow Two, go over there and investigate. Don't shoot at them; that man at your telephone probably doesn't know where the troops are. If they're Japs, run over them.

Yellow One, wilco.

Go ahead, Yellow Two. What in God's name are you waiting for?

I'm up as far as I can go and still depress my machine guns.

The hell with the machine guns! I told you to run over them! Run over them, goddammit; obey your orders!

Yellow Two, wilco. . . .

Yellow One, what have you to report on that machine gun?

Red One, a Jap stood up and threw a hand grenade at us so I gave him a squirt.

Did you run over that gun like I told you?

No. Red One, we put an HE [high explosive] in it and wrecked it.

Christ, won't you people ever learn to conserve your ammunition? . . .

Red One from Green Two. I'm stuck between two trees.

Green Three stand by him. After the infantry has cleared up around there, get your assistant driver out and tow him clear.

Green Three, wilco.

While you're waiting, Green Three, keep an eye on that house on your right. I see troops coming out of there stuffing bottles in their shirts.

Can I send my assistant driver over to investigate?

Stay in your tank.

Yellow One from Red Three, where are you going? . . .

Red One from Green Four. I am moving out to take a pillbox the infantry pointed out I will take care of it and let them catch up.

Where is it, Green Four?

In that clump of bushes to my right.

Can you see it? It is all right to fire? Wait, Green Four.

Green Four, wilco.

Green Four, you'd better not fire. The 4th Marines are over there somewhere.

Run up on the box and turn around on it.

It's one of those coconut log things. It looks like it might be too strong to squash. Is it all right if I fire in the slit?

Affirmative, but be careful, wilco. . . .

Red One, this is Hairless. We've got some Japs bottled up in two caves in Target Area Four Baker. We'd like you to leave two tanks to watch them.

You know damn well that's the infantry's work. We're a mobile outfit, not watchdogs. Put your saki drinkers in there.

OK, Harry. Red One, out.

All tanks, start 'em up. Move out now. Guide right and form a shallow right echelon. As soon as we hit the flat ground around the airfield, spread out to one-hundred-fifty yard interval. All right, move out, move out.

Among the many interesting accessories added to the M4 series tanks, were flamethrowers. This one, pictured here in operation, replaced the front-hull .30-caliber machine gun at the assistant driver's position. Flamethrowers saw limited use in the ETO, but were widely used in the Pacific in reducing fortified positions and jungle growth. *Patton Museum*

This staged photograph shows the crew of an M4 tank loading 75mm main gun rounds into its tank. The projectile portions of the rounds came in a variety of colors to assist the crew in telling them apart. Those in black with markings in white are M72 AP rounds. Olive drab paint and yellow markings indicates an M48 HE round. *Patton Museum*

CHAPTER THREE

FIREPOWER AND ARMOR PROTECTION

As cited in U.S. Army manuals from World War II, the M3 75mm gun mounted in the turret of the M4 series tanks was a single-shot flat trajectory weapon that fired four different types of ammunition. These rounds consisted of armor piercing (AP), high explosive (HE), white phosphorous (WP) nicknamed "Willy Pete," and canister.

Unlike artillery ammunition, which almost universally features adjustable powder charges that allow the trajectory to be varied to suit the mission, the 75mm rounds fired from the M4 series tank gun were all fixed. This meant the metal cartridge cases containing the primer and propelling charge were rigidly attached to the projectiles. This enabled the loader to insert them into the breech of the main gun in one swift motion.

Army manuals listed the official rate of fire of the 75mm main gun in the M4 series as 20 rounds per minute. Tom Sator, who fought in Northwest Europe with the 4th Armored Division during World War II, does not remember ever timing himself in action. However, on at least one occasion, he has no doubt that with his adrenaline pumping he might have reached somewhere between 15 to 20 rounds in a minute's time.

Allocation of ammunition types to be carried depended on anticipated missions of a tank, other supporting weapons (e.g. artillery, antitank guns, close air support), and in some cases, logistic availability of ammunition types.

Of the four types of main gun rounds fired from the M4 series tank, the M48 HE was the most used during World War II. The canister rounds saw use only against the Japanese. Jim Francis, a gunner with the 12th Armored Division in Northwest Europe, recalls that the majority of targets for his 75mm HE rounds were German 88mm and 75mm antitank guns.

Because there was almost no threat from Japanese tanks, U.S. Army and Marine Corps M4 series tankers in the Pacific theater of operations had little use for AP rounds and loaded their tanks primarily with HE.

Jim Carroll, who served as a gunner on a Marine Corps M4A3 tank during the Battle for Iwo Jima, recalls that the majority of rounds carried on his tank were HE, with some being canister and even fewer being AP, which he remembers never having fired. Canister rounds proved useful when encountering Japanese trenches, although

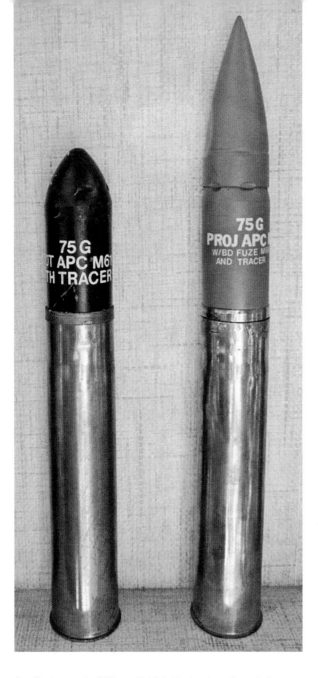

On display at the Military Vehicle Technology Foundation are two examples of the main gun rounds fired from the M3 75mm gun mounted on the M4 series of tanks. The round on the left is an M61 round. The one on the right is an M66A1 APC-T fitted with a base-detonating fuse intended to explode an HE filler, contained within the projectile, after penetration of a target. *Michael Green*

tankers seldom saw any Japanese soldiers during the fighting, as they tended to remain hidden in their extensive tunnel systems. The HE proved relatively ineffective against the stoutly built Japanese bunkers unless a lucky shot went into their very small and narrow firing ports.

Constructed of forged steel with comparatively thin walls, the M48 projectile contained 1.5 pounds of TNT.

It came with either a super quick (SQ) fuse or a delayed (0.05 or 0.15 seconds, depending on the model) point-detonating (PD) fuse. As shipped, all M48 series main gun rounds came with their fuse set for SQ. To change their fuse setting for PD, the loader turned a setting screw so that the slot aligned with the PD setting, which was at right angles to the axis of the fuse housing. Loaders could do this in the dark by noting the position of the slot in the setting sleeve.

The SQ fuse was prescribed against enemy personnel in the open, where the bursting projectile was more effective if it generated its lethal blast and fragments before burrowing into the ground. Delayed PD fuse allowed the projectile to penetrate targets, such as the light armor on antitank gun shields or buildings, before bursting. It was up to the tank commander or gunner to inform the loader what type of fuse setting to use before he loaded the round into the breech.

The M48 HE round came in two versions, with two different levels of propellant within their cartridge cases. There was the normal HE round, which weighed 18.8 pounds and had a muzzle velocity of 1,470 feet per second. Then there was the supercharge HE round that weighed 19.56 pounds and featured a muzzle velocity of 1,885 feet per second. As can be deduced, the supercharge HE round went farther than the normal HE round by 2,300 yards.

From an army wartime manual comes this description of the effectiveness of ricochet fire with the delay fuse on the HE round: "If the shell strikes the ground, it ricochets, travels 20 to 25 yards beyond the point of impact, and then bursts about 10 feet in the air. Because of the down-spray from the burst in the air, a ricochet burst has devastating effect on personnel without overhead cover."

The blunt-nosed canister round used in M4 series tanks came with the designation T30 and weighed 19.7 pounds. The projectile portion weighed 14.7 pounds. It was essentially a shotgun shell on steroids. A U.S. Army manual describes the canister round, "Canister consists of a light metal case filled with steel balls, containing no explosive. It is fired point-blank for effect against personnel. The case breaks upon leaving the muzzle of the cannon, allowing the balls to scatter with shotgun effect."

ARMOR-PIERCING (AP) ROUNDS

The heaviest complete round of main gun ammunition carried on the M4 series was the M61 APC-T (armor-piercing capped with tracer), which weighed about 20

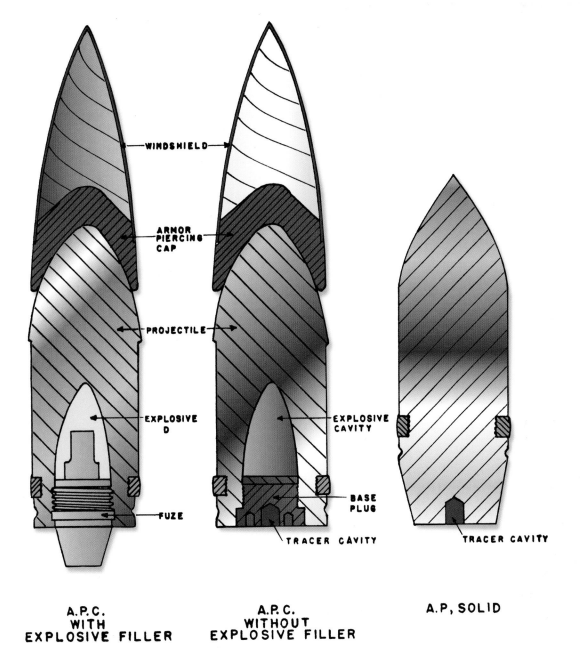

WINDSHIELD

ARMOR
PIERCING
CAP

PROJECTILE

EXPLOSIVE
D

EXPLOSIVE
CAVITY

BASE
PLUG

FUZE

TRACER CAVITY

TRACER CAVITY

A.P.C.
WITH
EXPLOSIVE FILLER

A.P.C.
WITHOUT
EXPLOSIVE FILLER

A.P, SOLID

This artwork illustrates three different types of 75mm main-gun AP rounds. AP solid (also known as shot) worked better than armor-piercing capped (APC) round against homogeneous steel armor at the lower obliquities. However, against face-hardened armor, APC projectiles had the advantage. The armor-piercing caps attached to the projectile noses of APCs assisted in overcoming face-hardened armor by protecting the main body of the projectile against shattering upon impact with its target. *James D. Brown*

pounds. The term "capped" referred to a forged steel alloy cap that fit over the normal steel nose of a projectile.

It seems intuitive that an armor-penetrating projectile should have a very sharp pointed nose, like the tip of a spear or a dagger. However, during a high-velocity impact, kinetic energy transfer through the tip of a sharply pointed projectile may occur over such a small area that the projectile shatters, like a sharp pencil point jabbed into a board. The job of the cap is to help relieve

initial stress on impact by spreading the energy transfer over a larger area and for a longer period of time, allowing the mostly undamaged projectile to penetrate the armor of an opponent's tank.

Because the ballistically optimal nose shape was rather blunt, the M61 APC-T's aerodynamic performance was poor. The characteristically high drag of a blunt shape degraded kinetic energy available at the target and resulted in arching trajectories, which in turn

German tank and antitank AP rounds were far superior to their American counterparts in both range and penetration. This left U.S. Army M4 series tankers at a huge disadvantage in combat. This particular M4 took an AP hit through its side-hull armor into the driver's compartment. *Patton Museum*

degraded the ability to obtain hits. To improve in-flight performance characteristics of the blunt-nosed APC-T projectile, a thin metal windshield (also known as a ballistic cap) attached to the front of the projectile.

AP projectiles having no high-explosive fillers were called "shot," a carryover from the days of Napoleonic muzzle-loading cannon, which could fire solid-shot or fused shell with explosive bursting charges. The M61 APC-T came with a small hollow cavity for the fitting of an HE filler. However, due to production problems the M61 went into service without the HE filler until the very end of World War II.

When the HE filler started showing up in the M61 APC-T rounds, they came with a base-detonating fuse that was supposed to detonate after penetration of a target had occurred. Conventional PD fuses affixed to the nose of the projectile would have been destroyed during initial impact and penetration, so the base-detonating configuration was necessary to ensure survival of the

fuse until penetration was complete. With the combination of the HE filler and base-detonating fuse, the M61 AP-T round became the M61 APC-HE-T. A later improvement, fitted with a different fuse, became the M61Al APC-HE-T.

The M61 APC-T round had a muzzle velocity of 2,030 feet per second. Muzzle velocity is the speed of the projectile as it leaves the muzzle of a gun. Faster projectiles are subject to external forces (e.g. gravity, cross-wind, etc.) for a shorter time, so they afford improvements in probability of obtaining a hit. Higher velocity also reduces the requirement for precise range estimation and simplifies the gunner's problem of lead estimation against moving targets. Kinetic energy of the projectile is a function of its mass and the square of its velocity, so faster projectiles are more lethal.

Besides the M61 APC-T or the M61Al APC-HE-T rounds, M4 tank gunners had another AP round available to fire—the M72 shot AP-T round. It weighed roughly 18

The penetrative powers of German AP projectiles are evident in these two photographs, which show the same tank from the front and rear. A number of German AP projectiles had passed clear through the front of the tank's hull and out the back. *Patton Museum*

pounds, of which the projectile portion weighed 13.94 pounds. The M72's muzzle velocity was the same as the M61, but its penetration capability suffered at increased range because absence of the ballistic cap meant its velocity degraded more on the way to the target.

Corporal James A. Miller, an M4 series gunner, described his frustrations with the apparent lack of muzzle velocity on his 75mm main gun in a wartime army report:

I have been in combat several times in a tank and I have found out it is silly to try to fight the German tank. One morning in Puffendorf, Germany, about daylight I saw German tanks coming across the field toward us; we all opened fire on them but we had just about as well have fired our shots straight up in the air for all the good we could do. Every round would bounce off and wouldn't do a bit of damage. I fired at one 800 yards away; he had his side toward me. I hit him from the lap of the turret to the bottom and from the front of the tank to the back directly in the side but he never halted. . . . In my opinion, if we had a gun with plenty of muzzle velocity we would have wiped them out. We out-gunned them but our guns were worthless.

The German Pz.Kpfw. IV Ausf. G's first encountered in North Africa had a roughly 10-foot-long rifled 75mm gun tube with a muzzle velocity of 2,427 feet per second, in comparison to the M4 tank's 2,030 feet per second. To make matters worse for the M4 tank gunners, the Pz.Kpfw. V (Panther) tank fired standard AP rounds downrange with velocities greater than 3,000 feet per second, as did the 88mm main guns on the Tiger I (also known as the Tiger E) and the Tiger B heavy tanks.

OPINIONS ON THE M4 SERIES AP

The M4 tank gunners could fire the M61 APC-T projectile a maximum range of 14,000 yards. Maximum range

Slugging it out with heavily armored German tanks was not the M4 series tank's intended job, as it was supposed to be a weapon of exploitation. Specially designed tank destroyers had the job of taking out German tanks. One of the most numerous was the M10 Tank Destroyer, based on the chassis of the M4 series tanks, and armed with a 3-inch gun. Another tank destroyer, the M36 Jackson, had a similar appearance. *Michael Green*

refers to the longest distance a projectile can travel, regardless of terminal effect. More important to tankers is the maximum effective range of a main gun and its ammunition, because it not only reflects the actual ability to hit the target, but also the projectile's capability to penetrate a target given a hit.

Most considered the maximum effective range of the M4 tank series 75mm AP ammunition to be grossly inferior to that of late-war German tanks. Captain Henry W. Johnson of the 2nd Armored Division, states his opinion in a wartime report: "The higher muzzle velocity of the German tanks enables them to far outrange our Sherman tanks. I have seen them knock our tanks out at ranges up to 1,000 yards and know no incident where a Sherman has knocked out a Mark V [Panther] or Mark VI [Tiger] at more than 300 yards."

Tank Commander Rains M. Robbins of the 2nd Armored Division is quoted in a wartime report saying, "In one recent action in which we took part, one of our medium tanks was hit and burned at a range of approximately 2,500 yards. In the same action, probably minutes later, we fired on and bounced several rounds of AP broadside off a Jerry tank at a range of 1,500 yards, and were unable to knock it out."

Corporal Francis E. Vierling, a tank commander in the 2nd Armored Division, describes the frustrations of being badly outgunned on the battlefield:

I believe the American M4 Sherman tank, a basically good implement of war, is beset by overwhelming disadvantages. . . . The greatest deficiency lies in its firepower, which is most conspicuous by

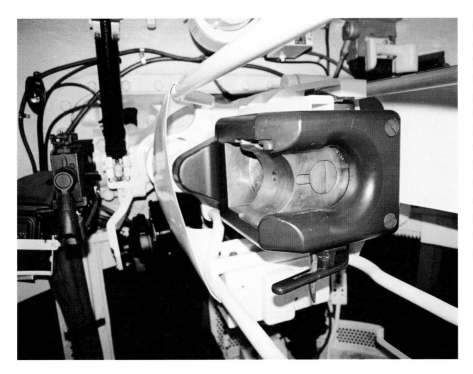

Clearly visible in this photograph of the interior of an M4 series tank turret is the breech mechanism of the M3 75mm gun, with the breechblock in the closed position. The primary purpose of a breech mechanism was to seal off the rear of a gun tube and align the firing pin against the base of the cartridge. A recoil guard (also called a body guard in army manuals) surrounds the breech mechanism. *Michael Green*

its absence. Lack of a principal gun with sufficient penetrating ability to knock out the German opponent has cost us more tanks and skilled men to man more tanks than any failure of our crews, not to mention the heartbreak and sense of defeat I and other men have felt. To see twenty-five or even many more of our rounds fired and ricochet off the enemy attackers. To be finally hit, once, and we climb from and leave a burning, blackened and now a useless pile of scrap iron. It would have yet been a tank had it mounted a gun.

WHAT HAPPENED?

How was it that the M4 tank series could be so ill-equipped, with a cannon and AP ammunition unable to penetrate the armor on late-war German tanks? On modern armored fighting vehicles, such as the American M1 Abrams main battle tank, the primary effectiveness of tank cannons comes from their ability to defeat the armor protection of other tanks. The M4 tank series first appeared in 1942, and the army envisioned its purpose as a deep-attack (exploitation) weapon, not as a tank-versus-tank combat vehicle. An example of this train of thought appears in an army manual dated April 1943: "The ultimate objective of the armored division is vital rear installations. These are attacked less with cannon than with the crushing power of the tank and with its

Early models of the M4 series lacked a direct-sight telescope (as did German tanks) and depended instead on an overhead periscope for the gunner, which contained a small magnified telescope within it. This meant there was no aperture opening in the gun or rotor shield, which is evident in this picture of an early production M4A1 tank with the M34 gun mount. *Patton Museum*

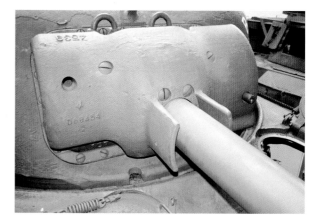

While waiting for production of the M34A1 gun mount, which featured an integral mount for a direct-view sighting telescope, builders of the M34 gun mounts took to modifying the aperture openings in the gun and rotor shields. Protection for the new aperture opening came from welding on an extra armor plate to the rotor shield, as seen in this photograph. These side-by-side pictures show the modified M34 gun mount on the left and the M34A1 gun mount on the right. *Jim Mesko*

machine guns. The main purpose of the tank cannon is to permit the tank to overcome enemy resistance and reach the vital rear areas."

To allow the M4 tank series to fulfill its primary mission as a weapon of exploitation, the army fielded highly specialized vehicles known as tank destroyers, which supposedly had cannons of sufficient power to penetrate any opposing enemy in a tank-versus-tank duel. The tank destroyer's job was to destroy enemy tanks attempting to block the M4 series tanks effort to plunge deep behind enemy lines. The idea that it took a specialized vehicle to destroy enemy tanks emerged within the senior ranks of the army in 1940.

General George C. Marshall, U.S. Army Chief of Staff in 1939, initiated the tank destroyer concept and General Lesley J. McNair nurtured it along. General McNair, appointed commanding general of the AGF in 1942, explains his position regarding the need for specialized tank destroyers, "Certainly it is poor economy to use a $35,000 medium tank to destroy another tank when the job can be done by a gun costing a fraction as much. Thus the friendly armored force is freed to attack a more proper target, the opposing force as a whole. . . ."

Due to this high-level support of the tank destroyer concept, it is understandable why doubters kept negative comments to themselves. It took combat reports to prove that the concept, referred to as combat doctrine by the military, was badly flawed. After the campaign in North Africa, General Ernest N. Harmon wrote, "There is no need for tank destroyers. I believe the whole

organization and development of the tank destroyer will be considered a great mistake of the war." Harmon was proved correct in his conclusion, as the tank destroyer branch disappeared from the army structure after World War II.

American tankers engaging German tanks in Northwest Europe in late 1944 and early 1945 quickly came to the same conclusion as many who saw combat earlier in North Africa. Colonel S. R. Hinds, of Combat Command B of the 2nd Armored Division, states in an early 1945 report that "in spite of the often quoted tactical rule that one should not fight a tank versus tank battle, I have done it almost invariably, in order to accomplish the mission."

Lieutenant Colonel Wilson M. Hawkins, commanding the 3rd Battalion, 67th Armored Regiment of the 2nd Armored Division, is quoted in the same report: "It has been stated that our tanks are supposed to attack infantry and should not be used tank vs. tank. It has been my experience that we have never found this ideal situation for in all our attacks we must of necessity fight German tanks. Therefore, it is necessary for a tank to be designed to meet adequately this situation."

In conclusion, the M4 tank series went into design and production with little or no forethought given to the need for the tank to engage other tanks. It was not for lack of trying, though. The Ordnance Department, responsible for the engineering development of tanks, kept pressing the AGF to increase the firepower on the M4 series to no avail until 1943.

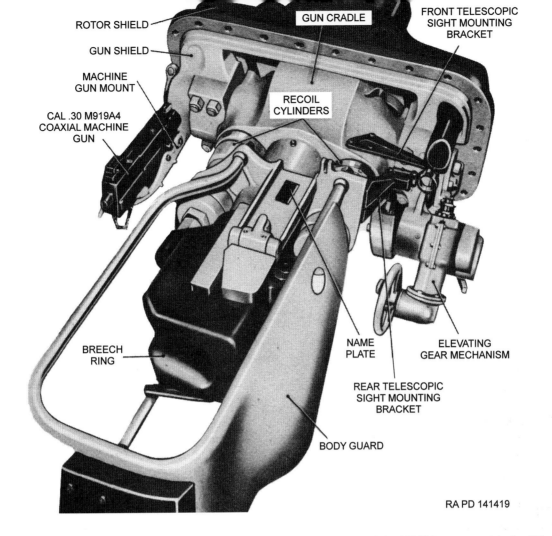

ROTOR SHIELD

GUN SHIELD

MACHINE GUN MOUNT

CAL .30 M919A4 COAXIAL MACHINE GUN

GUN CRADLE

FRONT TELESCOPIC SIGHT MOUNTING BRACKET

RECOIL CYLINDERS

BREECH RING

NAME PLATE

ELEVATING GEAR MECHANISM

REAR TELESCOPIC SIGHT MOUNTING BRACKET

BODY GUARD

RA PD 141419

From an army manual comes this illustration labeling all the various components of the M34A1 gun mount in the M4 series tanks. The purpose of the gun mount is to support and elevate the 75mm gun and the coaxial .30-caliber machine gun. The guns remain fixed in position relative to one another and cannot be traversed or elevated independently.

GUN TUBE AND ASSOCIATED COMPONENTS

Of the many components that made up the main gun on the M4 tank series, the most important proved to be its rifled gun barrel. A little more than 9 feet long, the 611-pound one-piece steel forging screwed into the 118-pound breech ring located inside the tank's turret.

The breech ring is the part of a barrel assembly, housing the mechanism that opens and closes, allowing for the insertion of rounds into an enlarged smooth-walled chamber. At its forward end, the chamber tapers down into a forcing cone, which allows copper rotating bonds on the projectiles to be engaged gradually by the gun tube rifling. Once fully engaged by the rifling, the projectile travels down the constant diameter bore toward the muzzle.

The chamber is always the thickest and strongest part of a gun tube, since the gas pressure caused by the rapid burning of the propellant contained within

the metal cartridge case is at its maximum within the chamber. When the primer and the propellant in a cartridge case ignite, the powder gases violently expand the cartridge case against the walls of the chamber and the breechblock. Trapped in this manner, the only escape for the rapidly expanding propellant gases is forward, which in turn drives the projectile out the bore of a gun tube at a very high velocity.

The breechblock is essentially a large heavy piece of steel, which closes and covers the back end of a gun tube. The M4 tank series breechblock was a horizontal-sliding type, with the upper front edge of the breechblock beveled to force a round into the firing chamber as the breech closed. A hole in the center of the breechblock housed a percussion firing mechanism, firing spring, and firing spring retainer.

The 75mm rifled gun tube on the M4 tank series, which contained and guided projectiles during their critical firing phase, sat in the central bore of a cradle that

Due to a shortage of electro-hydraulic power traverse units for the M4 series tanks, the Ordnance Department approved the fitting of a Westinghouse all-electric power traverse unit. This picture shows the interior of an M4A1 tank; the black handwheel controls traverse, while the white one controls elevation. *Chris Hughes*

allowed it to slide back and forth during recoil and counter recoil. The gun tube could not rotate in its cradle due to a breech ring key. The gun cradle on the M4 tank series had a trunnion on either side of it, and both of them functioned as an axis around which the cradle and the gun tube rotated in elevation. The trunnions rested in bearings on the inside of the front of the tank's turret.

On either side of the gun cradle were hydro-spring recoil cylinders that made up the M4 tank series' recoil mechanism. The hydro-springs controlled and limited the recoil of the main gun when fired and then returned the gun tube to its normal firing (battery) position. The hydro-spring recoil cylinders checked the movement of the recoiling mass in a gradual manner, preventing too strong an opposing force (shock) to the tank. Maximum recoil length on the 75mm main gun topped out at 14 inches, with the normal recoil length proving to be only 11 5/8 inches.

GUN MOUNT

The M4 tank series gun tube and the cradle formed part of the M34 gun mount located in the front wall of the turret. The M34 gun mount provided the structure needed to elevate or depress the gun tube and a mount for a coaxially mounted M1919A4 air-cooled .30-caliber machine gun fixed to fire alongside it. To elevate or depress the gun mount, the gunner used a vertically oriented hand-wheel located directly in front of his position in the turret. The hand wheel turned clockwise for elevating and counterclockwise for depressing.

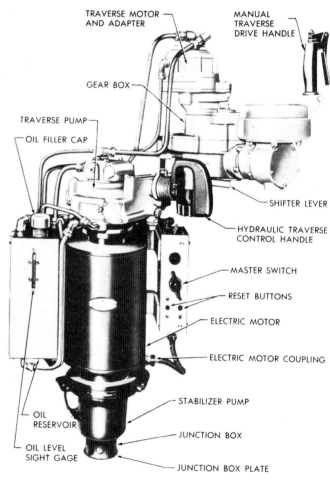

TURRET HYDRAULIC TRAVERSING MECHANISM

The various components that make up the preferred Oilgear Company electro-hydraulic power traverse unit are shown in this illustration from an army manual. There was also another less-preferred electro-hydraulic power traverse unit, built by the Logansport Company, and it was approved for use when Oilgear Company units were unavailable.

The electrical firing switches for the 75mm main gun and the coaxial .30-caliber machine gun in the M4 series tanks are shown in this illustration from an army manual. The gunner fired the 75mm main gun by stepping on the right switch with his left foot. He fired the coaxial machine gun by depressing the left switch. The pedal to the left of the firing switch box was a nonelectrical manual backup for firing the main gun.

An important part of the M34 gun mount was the cast-steel armored gun shield, which formed its exterior. The gun shield was attached with large bolts to the front turret wall of the tank. Two rounded lifting hooks were either welded or, as an alternate design, cast integrally to the top outer surface of the gun shield.

A narrow cast armored rotor shield (also known as a mantlet) protected the polished gun-tube bearing surface and prevented flying shrapnel and projectiles from entering the turret compartment. The mantlet had a machined bore through its center permitting the 75mm gun tube to extend through it and was fitted over the M34 gun shield. A separate and much smaller armored shield fit over the opening of the .30-caliber coaxial machine gun.

There was no opening for a gunner's telescope sight with the M34 gun mount, as the gunner depended on an overhead, indirect-view periscope that projected out the top of the tank's turret roof and in front of the tank commander's overhead hatch.

Desires for a direct-view telescope sight for the M4 tank series resulted in the new M34A1 gun mount, standardized in October 1942. This improved assembly incorporated a larger exterior armored rotor shield, the standard opening for the main gun in its center, a smaller opening on the left of the gun tube for the .30-caliber coaxial machine gun, and a similar small opening on the opposite side for the gunner's direct-view telescope sight.

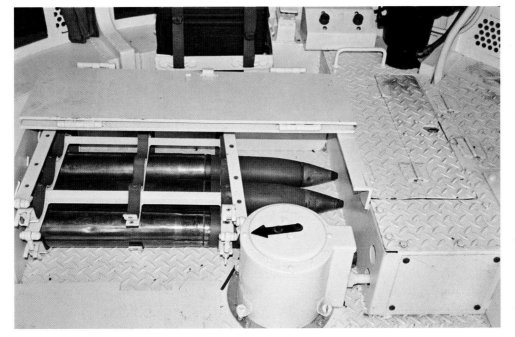

On the bottom of the turret basket of an M4A1 tank is the opened armor container that held eight main gun-ready rounds (only three rounds are shown here). U.S. Army manuals called for the loader to reserve these for emergencies, as they were the closer to him and the easiest to access in a hurry.
Michael Green

To the left of the loader in this M4A1 tank is one of the three armored ammunition storage containers for main-gun rounds within the vehicle's hull. The other two, not visible in this picture, would be on the other side of the hull and accessed by the gunner or tank commander, who then would pass main-gun rounds to the loader. The main-gun rounds stored behind the loader's position resided in horizontal racks, also accessed from the driver's position. *Michael Green*

To offset the increased weight of the armored rotor shield, a breech counterweight was added to the design.

Some of the M34 gun mounts were modified to use a direct-view telescope sight by welding on an armored extension to the right sight of the armored rotor shield to protect the telescope opening.

ROTATING THE TURRET

The minimum time required for traversing 360 degrees with either type of powered-traverse systems was 17 seconds. Joe Grieb, an M4 series gunner who served in Northwest Europe with the 4th Armored Division during World War II, remembers that once his tank commander spotted a target to their front or side and informed him of the direction of the target (either left or right).

It would normally take him no more than 5 or 6 seconds to acquire it in his gun sights using the tank's powered-traverse system.

To operate the electro-hydraulic power-traverse systems, which were the ones most commonly fitted to M4 series tanks, the driver turned on the vehicle's master switch. The gunner then turned on the battery master switch and then the traversing switch. This started the tank turret's electric motor and hydraulic pump. The gunner then gripped a vertically oriented pistol-grip control handle, positioned to the right of the gun elevating hand-wheel, and placed it in the power operating position.

By turning the pistol-grip control handle to the right, the M4 series turret traversed right, while turning

Located on the right side of M4 series tanks were two ammunition storage containers for the vehicle's main gun rounds, which faced each other. The main-gun ammunition storage container pictured is in an M4A1 tank, is located in the forward portion of the vehicle's hull, and holds seventeen main-gun rounds horizontally. *Michael Green*

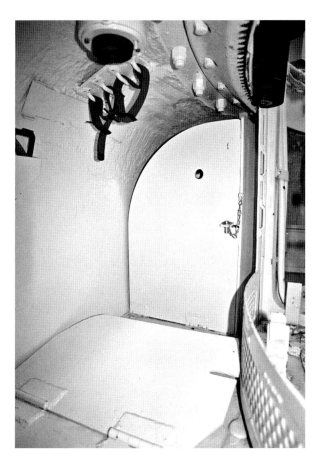

Nestled against the curve of the cast hull in the right rear side of this M4A1 tank, abutting up against the engine bulkhead, is a second armored storage container for main-gun rounds; in this case, it has the armored hatch door in the closed position. Behind this door resides storage space for fifteen main-gun rounds stored horizontally. Differences in hull shape between cast and welded variants contributed to differences in ammunition capacity between models. *Michael Green*

it to the left caused the turret to traverse left. Turret traverse speed was determined by how far the gunner turned the pistol-grip control handle. To stop the turret from traversing, the gunner released the control handle and the turret stopped automatically.

To rotate the turret manually, the gunner squeezed a lever on a vertical drive handle located on the top of a gear mechanism to the right of his seated position. Turning the drive handle clockwise rotated the turret to the right, while turning it counterclockwise turned it left. Releasing the hand lever on the vertical drive handle applied a brake in the hand traverse drive. It took the

gunner 296 complete rotations of the drive handle to traverse the tank's turret through 360 degrees.

On the right side of the gunner's position was a small turret lock wheel mounted on the turret ring. Use of the turret lock took loads off the traversing gears when turret motion was not needed. To lock the turret in position, the gunner turned the wheel clockwise as far as it would go. To unlock the turret, the gunner turned the wheel on the turret ring counterclockwise. Internal and, in some cases, external elevation locks were also used to take loads off the elevation gears.

ENGAGING A TARGET AND FIRING THE MAIN GUN

Many M4 series tank combat engagements began when the tank commander (with his head barely projecting out over the top of his open hatch for increased visibility) spotted a potential target, often with a pair of binoculars. Over the tank's intercom system, he verbally alerted the gunner by saying, "Gunner." He then provided the gunner a target description, for example, he said, "Tank."

Located below the turret basket floor and behind the assistant driver's seat was an armored container that held thirty main-gun rounds stored horizontally, with projectiles pointed to the rear. This photograph, taken inside an M4A1 tank, shows the opened thirty-round magazine, with the hull escape hatch just in front of it. *Michael Green*

This close-up photograph, taken inside an M4A1 tank, shows the gunner's two sighting instruments, the M70F direct-sight telescope on the left and the periscope M4A1 with telescope M38A2 on the right. Although the M70F telescope was a monocular instrument, it featured a full-face eye shield, which relieved the gunner's eye from strain by allowing him to keep both eyes open. *Michael Green*

This line drawing from an army manual shows the reticle pattern of the M70F direct-sight telescope mounted in an M4 series tank. It was graduated for the M61 APC round, which left the muzzle of the 75mm gun tube at 2,030 feet per second. When firing HE ammunition, which had a slower muzzle velocity, the gunner had to take up an adjusted sight picture.

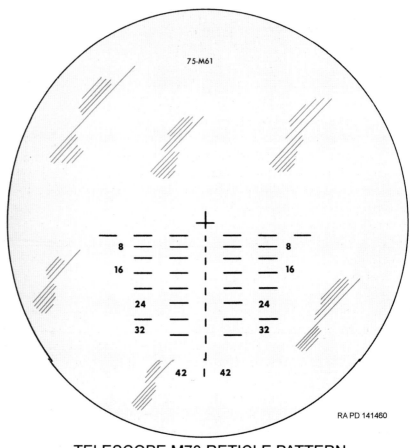

TELESCOPE M70 RETICLE PATTERN

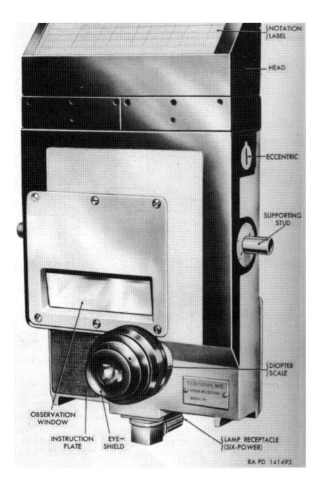

An illustration from an army manual shows an M10C periscope used in M4 series tanks. It contained a sight telescope that provided the gunner a six-power magnified image of the target, with reference marks located inside the instrument itself. Once seated in its mount, the periscope followed elevation motions of the gun cradle to maintain its relationship with the gun. By accurately superimposing the reticle image on the target, the gunner could establish an accurate line of sight to the target.

In the next moment, he announced to the loader and the gunner the type of main gun ammunition to load and fire, such as "AP," and sometimes "shot."

Tom Sator remembers that in his tank, the tank commander never had to tell him what to load. Once the tank commander had announced the type of target over the intercom, he had already begun loading the correct round in the gun and had at least two or three more ready to go, lying between his feet on the turret floor.

While the assumption that encounters with enemy tanks would always entail the use of AP projectiles only is prevalent, this was not always the case. First Lieutenant H. F. Hillenmeyer states in a wartime report regarding the fighting in North Africa: "In a scrap, we throw high explosive stuff until the enemy comes in range and then we change to armor piercing. Sometimes we set the high explosive for delay, fire low, and watch the Germans duck wildly as it ricochets over the ground."

Sergeant James H. Bowser, a tank commander in the 1st Armored Division, remarks in the same report, "A tank commander has got to remember that he can knock the track off a Mark IV long before he can hit it with armor piercing ammunition."

Second Lieutenant Thomas K. Bruce, a medium tank platoon commander in the 2nd Armored Division, states in a report: "On one occasion I obtained a complete penetration in one side and out the other of a turret on a Mark IV with a 75mm HE shell set on delay at about 100 yards range."

Even the M89 WP smoke rounds were used for destroying tanks. Tank Commander Ameth Anderson of the 2nd Armored Division, states in a wartime report, "Our smoke shell is very good on any target and I have found the Germans do not like it. I hit a Mk V [Panther] with AP five times, with HE four times at less than 1,000 yards, hitting him in the front and in the turret, and but one round of smoke did the trick by hitting him under his own gun mount."

The phosphorous in the M89 WP smoke rounds often ignited oil and grease deposits on enemy tanks, creating a surface fire, which could burn the target or cause smoke to enter into the vehicle through seams and joints, forcing the crew to abandon its vehicle, thus neutralizing it.

General George S. Patton's Third Army standard operating procedures (SOP) issued April 3, 1944, had this statement regarding the use of the M89 WP smoke round: "In tank versus tank duels, the first round should be armor piercing. If this fails, the second round must be white phosphorus and short to so as to give our tank a chance to maneuver, because by keeping its gun laid on the smoke, it has a better chance of getting in the second telling shot than has the enemy, who when he emerges from the smoke does not know the location of our vehicle."

LOADER'S ROLE

To load the main gun, the loader grasped and pulled on the breechblock's operating handle. As the breechblock opened to the right, extractors (levers) inside the breech ring were forced from their seated positions and locked

Pictured underneath an M4 series tank gun mount is the weapon's stabilizer. It held a tank's main gun and coaxial machine gun at a predetermined elevation while the tank was in motion. It had no control of movement in the horizontal plane due to the roll of the tank. *Michael Green*

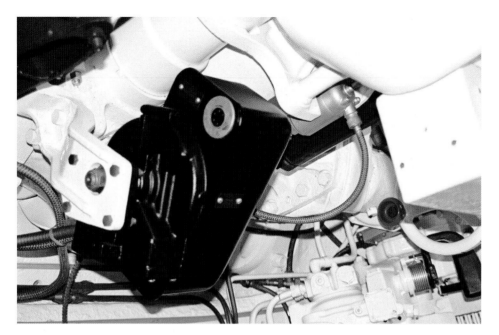

Located behind the gunner's manual turret traverse control handle in this M4A1 tank is the azimuth indicator. When the tank took part in the indirect fire mode, it was used in conjunction with a gunner's quadrant located on top of the interior gun mount. *Michael Green*

When the M4 series was in the design stage, the main German antitank gun was the 3.7cm Pak 35/36 seen here. It was the benchmark against which the armor design would be determined. *Michael Green*

the spring-loaded breechblock in the open position, ready to receive a round of ammunition. Normal practice for American tankers in World War II was to open the breechblock on their main gun once the order to move out came. This saved time in combat, often proving the difference between life and death.

Once the tank commander or gunner indicated the type of round to use on a target, the loader inserted the appropriate ammunition into the open breech as far as it would go, usually by pushing vigorously with the heel of his hand or his fist. As the rim of the case contacted the extractors, they unlatched the breechblock, which automatically closed it and cocked the firing pin. The loader then slid his hand away from the breech as the breechblock slammed shut. Upon firing, an operating cam attached to the gun mount seat opened the breech and ejected the now empty cartridge case (via the extractors) during the counter-recoil movement of the gun tube. As the extractors completed their travel, they once again latched the breechblock open, and the gun was ready to receive another round.

Following the ejection of the first cartridge case, the loader only had to insert the next round with sufficient force to cause the flange (rear rim) of the cartridge case to drive the extractors forward again. The side of each extractor had an inner projecting lip that fit between the rim of the cartridge case and the rear face of the gun tube when the breechblock closed.

Tom Sator remembers that depending on the information received on what type of targets they might encounter, either an AP or an HE round would be loaded into the main gun prior to entering into combat.

Jim Francis recalls that for safety reasons, nobody but the lead tank in a column could have a round already in the breech of the main gun and its machine guns loaded. This cost many tankers their lives due to the delay in loading their tank's weapons in combat.

Tom Sator recalls that he was taught in training to reach under the gun mount with his right leg and kick the gunner of the tank in the left shin to alert him that there was a main gun round ready to fire. This was the prescribed manner for the loader to alert the gunners to

A British soldier displays a captured German Panzerschreck (Tank Terror) with the rocket it fired. The Panzerschreck was merely an enlarged copy of the American military M1 Bazooka, which could penetrate a little more than 6 inches of steel armor sloped at angle of up to 60 degrees. *Patton Museum*

a round in the breech. Jim Francis never waited for that kick to the shin from his loader and fired immediately upon hearing the breechblock slam shut on a main gun round in the chamber of his tank's 75mm gun.

GUNNER'S ROLE

As soon as the tank commander announced the target and the type of main gun ammunition to use, he informed the gunner the direction to traverse the turret to acquire the target by announcing, "Gunner traverse right!" or "Gunner traverse left!" Since the field of view from the gunner's sights is very limited, the tank commander often guided the gunner until the target was in his

view, such as "Gunner steady . . . steady . . . on!" The word "steady" informed the gunner to slow down the traverse rate of the tank's turret, as he was almost on the chosen target. The M4 series gunner used the manual elevation controls to fine-tune his aim on a target.

Jim Carroll recalls that, in his tank, the tank commander normally just shouted his last name over the intercom, and said to swing either right or left and look for a certain bush or clump of dirt.

To assist the tank commander in obtaining a rough aim on a target, a small vertical metal vane sight was mounted on the turret roof, in front of the periscope located in his overhead hatch. By aligning this sight with a somewhat larger corresponding vane sight located forward of the gunner's overhead periscope sight, the tank commander could sometimes "talk" the gunner toward the chosen target.

Once the gunner spotted the target in his sight, he was to announce over the tank's intercom system, "Target identified!" This was part of a series of prescribed oral communications protocol that the U.S. Army insisted that all tank crews used. More often, though, in the heat of battle and as the fear crept in, the crews reverted to using a much simpler form of oral communications between themselves. Tom Sator remembers that instead of hearing "target identified" from the gunner, more than often, he heard, "I see the goddamn thing!" or "I see it! I see it!"

On early production units of the M4 series tank, the gunner relied on the M4 periscope-type gun sight, which incorporated a 1.44-power M38 telescopic sight on its right side. The upper portion of this sighting system projected out of the top of the M4 series turret roof, and this arrangement eliminated the need for an extra opening in the gun shield and a potential ballistic weak spot in the armor. However, the articulated linkage between the gun sight and the gun mount itself often fell out of alignment, causing gunners to miss their targets during the fighting in North Africa in late 1942 and early 1943. A later improved version of this sighting system was the M4A1 periscope gun sight, which incorporated the telescope M38A2 and which featured a different reticle pattern than the older M38 telescope sight.

The army's dissatisfaction with the original sighting arrangement on the M4 series tank is evident in this quote from a March 1, 1943, report from the 1st Armored Division having fought in North Africa: "We must have a better sight for our guns, something with a four power to six telescopic power and something focusable. The sight should have a larger reticle and it must be illuminated for night fighting. This is extremely important; it should be changed immediately."

To correct the problem with the M4 periscope-type gun sight (incorporating a telescope sight), later production units of the M4 series tanks received a new three-power direct-sight telescope in the fall of 1942. During the winter of 1942–1943, several new telescopes with better optical characteristics were developed, and in July 1943, the army standardized the telescope M70F for the M4 series tanks. The M70F telescope was the same size and magnification as the earlier telescopes but featured superior optical quality.

The three-power M70F telescope was tubular in shape, measured 22 inches in length, and was illuminated by an instrument light. Etched within the telescope was a simple ballistic reticle customized for ammunition type, with vertical lines representing various ranges and horizontal lines used as lead lines for applying corrections for the motion of a target across the line of sighting.

The horizontal range lines inside the M70F telescope also added the super-elevation needed for gunners to hit a target accurately. Super-elevation is the angle above the line of sight needed to compensate for the effects of gravity during the projectile's time in flight.

All of the various types of direct-sighting telescopes incorporated into the M4 series turret mounted on two brackets, located on the right sight of the main gun mount, and the telescope moved with it as it elevated or traversed. To minimize the danger of a projectile passing down the telescope opening in the M34A1 rotor shield and harming the gunner, the aperture on the exterior of the rotor shield was no larger than the rotor shield opening for the coaxial .30-caliber machine gun.

How did the telescope sight in the M4 series tank compare to its German counterpart? According to Sergeant Lewis A. Taylor in a wartime report, "The German telescopic sight mounted in their tanks is superior to ours, in particular it is more powerful, in fact all of their optical equipment is superior to ours." Howard A. Wood, a gunner on an M4 series tank fighting in Northwestern Europe, states in the same report, "The telescopic sight on the Mark V [Panther] is also better than ours, because it always has a lever to make the sight have six-power or two, whichever is needed."

Periscope-type gun sights appeared on all M4 series tanks, as well as the M4 series-derived M10 tank destroyers, and remained as backup for the direct-sight telescopes. The M10 series periscopes featured a high-powered telescope on the right side for sighting distant targets and a periscope with a projected reflex reticle on the left side for sighting nearby targets.

HITTING THE TARGET

Modern main battle tanks feature laser rangefinders that provide the exact range to a target in a fraction of a second. Range estimation during World War II was almost entirely dependent on the skill and experience of the tank commander and the gunner. Once the tank commander announced to the gunner his estimated range to a target, the gunner centered the image of the target at the intersec-

Taking aim with Panzerfaust (Tank Fist) is a young German soldier. Unlike the American bazooka and the Panzerschreck, this weapon was a one-shot affair, thus discarded after firing. The weapon's shaped-charge warhead could penetrate close to 8 inches of steel armor sloped at 30 degrees at a range of roughly 50 yards. *Patton Museum*

tion of the horizontal and vertical lines showing the proper range and deflection on the ballistic reticle pattern.

When the tank commander gave the order to fire the 75mm main gun, the gunner called out, "Ready!" (according to army training manuals), then moved his head clear of the optical sight. At the same time, he depressed with his left foot one of two foot-operated electrical switches in a switch box attached to the turret basket floor. Prior to this moment, the gunner should have thrown a firing switch in a control box to the "on" position.

Of the two foot-operated switches, the right switch energized the main gun firing solenoid, while the left one energized the firing solenoid for the coaxial .30-caliber machine gun. If the electrical method failed to fire, there was a backup floor-mounted firing pedal in the turret basket to the left of the switch box.

Jim Carroll remembers that it was standard practice in his tank for him to fire the coaxial machine gun at what he believed was the target. This provided the tank commander (observing the fire) the input he needed to make sure the correct target was in his sights.

Joe Grieb recalls that he often did not wait for his tank commander to issue an order to fire on an enemy target and opened fire as soon as he had a clear shot in his optical sights.

Jim Francis recounts how waiting for the tank commander to give fire commands often took too long. It was quicker and more efficient to give the loader instructions on what type of main gun round to load when Francis spotted a target. He would indicate to the loader the round type desired by giving hand signals under the gun mount. A fist informed the loader that he wanted an AP round. Five spread fingers meant that the loader should insert an HE round.

In General Patton's Third Army SOP, a statement in the Tank Gunnery section instructs, "It is of the utmost importance that tank crews, particularly the commander and the gunner, be trained to get a hit with the first shot against surprise targets such as antitank guns or enemy tanks."

If the first round failed to find its mark, the tank commander or gunner observing (sensing) the fall of the projectile would adjust the barrel to a new position for the second round, and so on until the target sustained a hit, or hits, capable of rendering it inoperable. The loader would continue to load the type of round first ordered unless the tank commander or gunner changed his mind or ordered, "Cease fire!" Sometimes gunners could not estimate the range to their target after the first round fired, because the dust and smoke created by the muzzle blast from their 75mm gun obscured their view.

An example of the problem of obscuration effects on the crews when firing is related in this quote from a wartime report: "I'm a gunner on a Sherman tank which mounts a 75mm gun. When the wind is blowing in the right direction while the round is being fired, we are unable to sense the round being fired. This is due to muzzle blast and smoke, which comes from the gun. This same muzzle blast makes us slow to fire at targets

To counter the shaped-charge warheads of the Panzerschreck and the Panzerfaust, American tankers began adding a wide range of objects to their vehicles. The handmade standoff armor provided some means of predetonating or diffusing a shaped-charge warhead as it struck their vehicle. The most common form of protection for M4 series tanks proved to be sandbags, as pictured here on this tank carrying a squad of infantrymen. *Patton Museum*

at extreme ranges because it immediately gives our position away."

At shorter ranges, the American military expected tank gunners to hit the target with the first shot solely by means of the reticles in their sights. At longer ranges of 1,000 yards or more (or when visibility was poor), "bracketing" proved to be the preferred method for striking a target. Bracketing is a method of adjusting fire by forming an imaginary bracket around an enemy target. This is accomplished by firing over a target and in front of the target along a spotting line, and then correcting the aiming point by splitting the imaginary bracket in half until the target sustains a hit.

IMPROVING THE ODDS OF HITTING A TARGET

To assist the gunner in combat, the 75mm main gun along with the coaxial .30-caliber machine gun featured a stabilizer. It allowed the gunner to fire his turret

weapons when the tank was moving by keeping them at a predetermined vertical elevation. The stabilizer had no control of movement in a horizontal plane due to roll or changes in direction or movement. Even if a second reference gyroscope had been added to enable two-axis stabilization, the technology of the time would not have permitted rapid slewing of the turret.

The stabilizer consisted of a number of components, one of the most important being the gyroscope (gyro). Gyroscopes are based on a rapidly spinning wheel whose rotational momentum establishes a reference plane that is independent of vehicle motion. If sensors attached to the gyro detect displacement of the gun with respect to the gyro reference plane, signals are sent to the hydraulic system, which controls the elevation of the gun, to keep the gun pointed in a fixed position in space.

Because the M4 series single-plane gyrostabilizer could not control turret azimuth, it did not allow for true shoot-on-the-move capability. It did, however, sta-

While sandbags might have provided a measure of added protection from shaped charged warheads, it provided almost no protection from German high-velocity AP projectiles, as is evident in this picture of an M4 tank that suffered a penetration in the lower front hull. *Patton Museum*

bilize the gunner's two sets of sights, so he could see targets at longer ranges without the constant motion as the vehicle moved.

Use of the stabilizer did allow the tank's gunner to direct more accurate fire from his .30-caliber coaxial machine gun in some situations. In the case of the machine gun, uncorrected lateral movement due to motion of the tank would horizontally distribute the beaten zone (the area on the ground where rounds will land), which was often desirable when firing at infantry concealed in trench lines or hedgerows. The crew sometimes resorted to main gun firing on the move, but hit probability was so poor that it did little more than keep the enemy's head down, and bolster the morale of the crew until a suitable stationary firing position could be found.

An army manual, titled *Armored Forces Field Manual, Tank Gunnery*, and published in 1943, made this statement: "Firing with the 75mm gun while moving is inaccurate and causes an uneconomical expenditure of ammunition; do it only in an emergency and at ranges of 600 yards and under."

Jim Francis recounts that while on level terrain the stabilizer might have proven useful. On rough terrain, the gunner and loader were bouncing up and down so much while the sights were not, thus making it impossible for the gunner to keep his eye glued to his sight and for the loader to inset a round in the breech. Tom Sator believes that the stabilizer system on his tank was one of the few advantages they had over German tanks, which had to stop to fire accurately. By being able to fire on the move made his tank just that much harder to be hit by German tankers.

Earl W. Norris, who drove a very large tow truck and spent all his time fixing M4 series tanks for the 12th Armored Division during World War II, remembers that it was nearly impossible to keep the stabilizer systems working properly and, as a result, very few tankers used them.

INDIRECT FIRE

Besides its employment in the direct-fire mode, the M4 series was equipped with the instruments needed to fire the 75mm main gun in the indirect-fire role, like an artillery piece. However, medium- and high-velocity tank guns were generally ill-suited for this purpose, due to their lack of adjustable powder charges. Furthermore, the limited elevation angle available in their mounts meant the tanks had to drive onto prepared earthen berms to achieve the needed elevation angles. Still, unavailability of artillery sometimes occasioned the need for M4 series tanks to perform an indirect-fire role.

Because the gunner's sights could not be used to lay the gun onto the required azimuth and elevation for indirect fire, additional equipment was needed. A calculated solution—determined from a map (to ascertain distance and azimuth) and firing tables (to establish elevation)—was required. Azimuth is the horizontal angle between an object and a reference direction. For M4 series indirect-fire missions, azimuth was measured by the M19 azimuth indicator.

The M19 azimuth indicator was attached to the upper portion of the turret basket just behind the gunner's right elbow. To prepare for an indirect-fire mission, the tank commander had to determine a reference direction, usually from a compass or by inspecting a map. Once the reference direction was determined, the gunner traversed the turret to point in the reference direction and set the

Forming part of the massive collection of armored fighting vehicles of the Military Vehicle Technology Foundation are the two tanks pictured. On the left is an **M4A1** tank in the marking of the U.S. Army's 4th Armored Division, and on the right its German wartime counterpart, the Pz.Kpfw. IV, armed in this case with a long-barrel high-velocity 75mm main gun. *Michael Green*

adjustable pointers on the M19 to read that direction. Subsequent fire commands included a firing azimuth, which the gunner implemented by traversing the turret until the desired reading showed on the instrument. Before the end of the war the M19 azimuth indicator was replaced with an improved version designated the M20.

A device known as the elevation quadrant was located on the top of the interior gun mount at the gunner eye level. It established the required vertical angle to which the 75mm main gun must be elevated or depressed for indirect fire. This vertical angle was composed of two elements, the angle of super-elevation and the angle of site. The super-elevation angle was determined from firing tables and gave the horizontal range to the target, while the angle of site was applied to the main gun and corrected the differences in altitude between the firing site and the target site.

Angle-of-site calculations required the tank commander to determine the trigonometric arctangent of

the ratio of the difference in altitude between the tank and the target, divided by the horizontal range. It can be seen that, in an age before electronic calculators, efficacy of this engagement technique was limited by the number of tankers who were proficient in using a slide rule. Additionally, whenever the tank was driven onto a berm to achieve the needed elevation, the plane of reference of the azimuth indicator also rotated in space, causing it to give erroneous readings. Although all these computations were well within the capabilities of the field artillerymen who performed indirect fire as their stock-in-trade, it is easy to see that the indirect-fire capabilities of tanks were more hypothetical than practical.

ARMOR PROTECTION

Lieutenant Colonel Wilson M. Hawkins, who fought in North Africa and Northwest Europe, shares his impression of the armor protection level of the M4 series in a wartime report: "I have inspected the battlefield at Faid

Despite the widespread belief in the American military that the M4 series tanks was prone to exploding and burning upon being penetrated by a projectile, it was actually the propellant in the main gun cartridge cases that exploded upon penetration by any type of projectile fragment, as is seen in this photograph. The difference was only of academic interest to crewmen. *Patton Museum*

Pass in Tunisia, being with the force which retook it. Inspection of our tanks destroyed there indicated that the 88mm gun penetrated into the turret from the front and out again in the rear. Few gouges were found indicating that all strikes had made penetration. Our tanks were penetrated by 88, 75, and 50mm in this engagement in all parts of the hull and turret."

There were numerous reasons for the lack of heavier armor on the M4 series. Armor is the heaviest element of any tank design. Steel armor plate that is 1 inch thick weighs 40 pounds per square foot. When the M4 series came about, the engineers were constrained by the weight limit of 35 tons, because cranes fitted to the majority of transport ships could not load or unload anything heavier. Portable bridges employed by the U.S. Army in the early days of the war also had an upper weight-bearing limit of around 35 tons.

Due to the need to produce a tank with a turret-mounted 75mm gun as quickly as possible, the M3 medium tank chassis and engine became the basis for the M4 series. While this decision certainly sped up the M4 series design and production, it saddled the designers with a number of design problems, such as figuring

out the minimum amount of armor protection needed by the tank to carry out its battlefield roles.

The Ordnance Department learned the main antitank weapon of the German infantry in 1941 was a towed 37mm antitank gun. It fired an AP round that, in theory, could penetrate 2.2 inches (56 millimeters) of steel armor at a range of 220 yards. Therefore, the armor protection on the M4 series came out thick enough to stop an AP round fired from the German 37mm antitank gun.

In the Pacific area of operation, the Marine Corps tankers found that their M4 series tanks were almost completely impervious to anything but a lucky hit from the standard Japanese Army towed antitank gun, the 37mm Type 94, which was a copy of the German Army 37mm antitank gun. A larger 47mm Japanese towed antitank (designated the 47mm Type 1) proved a more potent threat to M4 series tanks in the Pacific Ocean area of operation. Luckily, the Japanese industrial base did not have the resources to build enough of them to meet all the needs of the Japanese Army.

What the American tank designers had failed to foresee when laying out the tanks' armor protection levels during World War II were the amazing advances the German military was making in antitank weapon technology, which eventually left the American tanks badly underprotected. While many stopgap measures appeared, both officially and unofficially as field modifications, none really could meet the expectations of the American tankers.

From the book titled *Come Out Fighting: The Epic Tale of the 761st Tank Battalion, 1942–1945*, written shortly after World War II, Trezzvant W. Anderson describes the fear that faced all M4 series tankers going into combat:

This was the moment for which all that training back in the USA had been aimed. There still lingered a slight catch in the throats of all. Everybody was thinking; the inside of a tank is a heluva place to be, when red hot, white hot steel fragments from an armor-piercing shell are ricocheting around, and just can't go anywhere else but the inside of the tank. God, how those things would tear the insides out of a man, spilling them all over the clean white walls of the tank, and its glistening floors! And, the hellish part about it was the fact that once it got in there, there just wasn't a dammed thing you could do about it!

Tom Sator could never understand why they painted the inside of American tanks white. When his tank lost its first tank commander to a very small artillery fragment that went through his helmet, his corpse dropped inside the tank's turret and splattered his brains and blood all over the inside of the vehicle. They could not get the bloodstains out of the tank's interior, no matter how hard they tried.

INFANTRY ANTITANK WEAPONS

In the European Theater of Operations, AP projectiles fired from guns accounted for up to 50 percent of all tank losses. However, as the fighting progressed, the proportion of tank losses due to shaped-charge weapons increased from 10 percent to 35 percent. This was due largely to the ever-increasing profusion of handheld infantry antitank weapons with shaped-charge warheads (also referred to as HEAT, an acronym for high-explosive antitank) issued to German military units beginning in 1944. These included the Panzerschreck (Tank Terror) and the Panzerfaust (Tank Fist).

A shaped-charge warhead penetrates armor by focusing its explosion onto a conical metal liner—usually copper—and causing it to extrude into a narrow jet with a velocity of tens of thousands of feet per second. The resulting penetration of the high-speed copper stream erodes metal spall particles from the armor itself that move at very high velocities. The white-hot copper and armor particles, along with residual blast carried through the perforation, constitute the main hazard to the crew. The shaped-charge penetration process lasts a few millionths of a second, after which it dissipates very quickly.

Tom Sator recalls how a German Panzerfaust penetrated the hull on the gunner's side of his tank, taking off a chunk of the gunner's left calf and impacting just below his seat. The resulting blast and overpressure wave hurled him and the tank commander straight out of their respective overhead hatches and onto the ground beside their tank. The only thing that saved them from having broken bones was the thick blanket of snow on the ground in January 1945. After coming to their senses and removing the wounded gunner from their disabled tank, Tom noticed that his leather seat cover looked like a very large tiger had pulled its claws across it. He felt lucky to have survived that encounter.

Besides using intense suppressive fire to force the Panzerfaust gunners to keep their heads down, M4 series crews developed a number of other defensive measures to reduce the effectiveness of the Panzerfaust.

This photograph shows an M4A3 tank that suffered a catastrophic detonation of its onboard main-gun ammunition, the force of which displaced the vehicle's turret from the hull. Fire had also ravaged the vehicle, destroying the ballistic integrity of the tank steel armor and making rebuilding impossible. *Patton Museum*

A field-expedient way to beef up their thin armor was to find spare tracks, sandbags, wooden logs, planks, and any other materials and secure them to the vehicles.

All of these add-on items acted as a form of standoff armor to predetonate the shaped-charged warheads of the Panzerschreck and Panzerfaust before they actually struck the vehicle's armor. Although it did not always work, it worked often enough to convince many M4 series crews to load down their vehicles with a wide variety of different materials. On occasion, the handmade standoff armor also diverted AP projectiles.

Author Belton Y. Cooper, in his book titled *Death Traps: The Survival of an American Armored Division in World War II*, describes what he saw while he was an ordnance officer in Northwest Europe, between the summer of 1944 and the end of the war in Europe. In this excerpt, he writes about what happened when an M4 series tank had the misfortune of having a Panzerfaust high-explosive jet penetrate its armor and strike a crew member: "When a tanker inside a tank received the full effect of a penetration, sometimes the body, particularly the head, exploded and scattered blood, gore, and brains throughout the entire compartment. It was a horrible sight. The maintenance crews had to get inside and clean up the remains. They tried to keep the body parts together in a shelter half and turn them over to graves registration. With strong detergent, disinfectant, and water, they cleaned the interior of the tank as best they could so men could get inside and repair it."

Jim Francis remembers how after losing their first tank, they were given another in which the tank commander had been killed. Ordnance had cleaned it as best they could, but they could not get all the blood out of the under-floor. When things got warm inside the tank, a sickening odor would drift up from below reminding them of what may lay in their future.

Antitank mines accounted for about 10 percent of tank losses. During the attempt to wrest control of the island of Iwo Jima from the Japanese Army in early 1945, Marine Corps tankers (now equipped with the M4A3 tank) dealt with a wide variety of antitank mine threats. Kenneth W. Estes, in his book titled *Marines Under Armor: The Marine Corps and the Armored Fighting Vehicle, 1916–2000*, describes this incident: "As the troops neared the second of the [Japanese] airfields, the V Corps approved Lieutenant Colonel Collins' plan for massing of all three tank battalions to overrun this prize. Attacking on D+5, the plan failed as the tanks drove over the largest concentration of mines

encountered to date, including many aerial torpedoes and sea mines turned into antitank mines. These oversize explosive devices shattered entire M4A3 tanks, sending their crews flying in the air, and a few of these tankers even managed to live through the experience."

HE projectiles caused approximately 5 to 10 percent of tank losses. According to a postwar army report, "One of the most vulnerable to the blast effect of high-explosive projectiles is the hull roof of tanks, at the joint between the turret and the hull roof. . . . Air inlet well covers, hatch doors and latches, periscope holders, and other such components are especially vulnerable to blast."

In his book titled *Another River, Another Town: A Teenage Tank Gunner Comes of Age in Combat—1945*, author John P. Irwin describes the effectiveness of HE, "One thing about HE was its concussion, which could incapacitate turret mechanisms, tracks, and other moving parts, even if the shell failed to penetrate the armor. Tanks could be completely disabled this way."

Of the total Allied tank losses during World War II, about 40 percent burned. In general, hull penetration on tanks caused more fires than turret penetrations, due to the fact that the fuel tanks and main gun ammunition for tanks were located in the hull.

AMMUNITION FIRES

One of the earliest protection problems on the M4 series was the tank's propensity to burn when struck by various antitank projectiles. An army observer in the North African campaign states in a report, "I examined approximately four-hundred non-repairable, battle-damaged armored vehicles, mostly light and medium tanks. . . . 95 percent of the non-repairable tanks had burned out."

So serious was the problem of fires with the M4 series that the Germans nicknamed the British versions as the "Tommy Cooker" (Tommy was slang for British soldier). American tankers nicknamed their M4 series tanks the "Ronson," after a small portable handheld cigarette lighter of the day, "guaranteed to light first time," as advertising of the time claimed.

Tom Sator still remembers to this day the very unpleasant stench of burnt human flesh emanating from the blackened hulks of his friends' tanks. The fear of being inside a burning M4 series tank was so great that American tankers wasted no time when disembarking from their vehicles when struck.

In an army report, dated June 6, 1945, and titled "Observations on Problems in Armor Units," the following statement relates how tanks were struck and burned and the psychological toll it took on the crews: "The . . . effects of burnouts have been quite uniformly bad. Two or three burnouts appear to be the maximum tolerated by the average man. A very few have stood six or eight without breaking, especially when two or three have occurred the same day. . . . Experience has been that a man is never again entirely effective after the first breakdown; after the second which occurs in from 30 to 50 percent of cases he becomes unusable, which is a command function."

THE REAL REASON FOR AMMUNITION FIRES

Many American tankers fighting in North Africa blamed the fires that consumed their tanks on the gasoline fuel used to power them. An example of this feeling appears in a quote from a report dated March 1, 1943, from the 1st Armored Division: "Gasoline-powered tanks are regarded by their crews as fire-traps. The men greatly prefer the less inflammable diesel powered tank."

Despite their belief that it was the gasoline fuel that made their M4 series tanks burn so easily, it instead proved to be the main gun ammunition stored within them that caused the fires. A British officer comments in a wartime report, "Self-sealing gasoline tanks for tanks are nice, but they are not vital. It is the ammunition, not the gasoline that burns. German tanks burn too if ammunition is hit. I think that the Germans aim to hit our ammunition. In one battalion 15 tanks were penetrated; 11 of them burned, 10 because of ammunition. . . . In another battle 15 tanks were penetrated; 7 burned, all but 1 by ammunition fire."

Once a projectile of most any type penetrated the armor of an M4 series tank hull, it would often strike the main gun ammunition racks (primarily located in the hull sponsons), ignite the propellant charges contained within the metal cartridge cases, and begin to burn within a few seconds. In most cases, this happened before the crew could evacuate their vehicle. On the original M4 series tanks, the majority of the 75mm main gun rounds were stored within light-sheet steel boxes, with another twelve stored vertically in clips along the inside wall of the turret basket for easy access by the loader.

The U.S. Army's answer to the problem of propellant fires within M4 series involved a number of fixes. First was the elimination of the twelve 75mm main gun round clipped to the wall of the turret basket. This meant that the authorized number of main guns in the

Clearly visible in this photograph of a Canadian Army M4A2 tank are the prominent hatch hoods for the driver and the assistant driver. Combat experience soon showed the vertical front of the hatch hoods on welded hull tanks were a ballistic weak spot. The antenna in the front hull of this tank identifies it as a command tank. *George Bradford collection*

M4A1 dropped to seventy-eight, and in the welded hull M4, M4A2, M4A3, they dropped to eighty-five.

Next, all the thin sheet steel main gun ammunition storage containers disappeared. In their place appeared similar-sized containers constructed of 1/4-inch thick steel armor plate. This added safety feature was rendered somewhat useless by the fact that both U.S. Army and Marine Corps tankers often carryied extra rounds within their tanks for fear of running out at an inopportune time.

According to M4 series tank authority Joe DeMarco, his research has uncovered that the armoring of the main gun ammunition storage containers for M4 series tanks began on the production lines around August 1943. Field modification kits, known as "quick fix," were also supplied in sufficient numbers to Great Britain, so that just about every early to mid-production M4 series tank that needed the kit got it before the invasion of France—D-day—on June 6, 1944.

As another stopgap measure to prevent main gun ammunition fires, 1-inch-thick steel armor plates began appearing on the exterior of M4 series tank hulls opposite the sponson ammunition racks. These add-on plates would disappear from later production vehicles, as the armor in those areas were thickened. Additional protective features for the main-gun ammunition storage on the M4

To remedy the hatch hood problem on welded-hull M4 series tanks, the Ordnance Department ordered that 1 1/2-inch homogenous steel armor sections be welded in front of the hatch hoods at a slight angle to bring them up to the same level of protection as the rest of the tank's front hull. This is clearly visible on this image of an M4A4 tank. *Michael Green*

series showed up on an improved second generation of the vehicle, which did not enter service until 1944.

OTHER WEAK SPOTS

In early production M4 series tanks equipped with the electric turret power traverse system, part of the interior turret wall in front of the gunner's position had been machined away to provide more room for the gunner when operating his controls. Combat experience, however, showed this to have been a serious mistake. British tank units fighting in North Africa in 1942 first reported it. It was also mentioned in a March 1, 1943, report from the 1st Armored Division: "The frequency of penetration by enemy shell-fire on the turret of the M4 tank indicates that the recess of indentation formed thereon for the fitting of appliances has dangerously weakened the vehicle's armor in a critical area."

As a result of this report, these tanks were fitted with add-on armor plate on the right front of their turrets beginning in the summer of 1943. This feature later disappeared as the foundries making the turrets thickened up that section of the turret.

Combat experience had shown that the driver and assistant driver's hatch hoods, which protruded from the front of welded-hull M4 series tanks (the M4, M4A2, M4A3, and M4A4) were a ballistic weak point. To correct this problem, the vertical surfaces on the front of these hoods had 1 1/2-inch-thick steel armor plates welded on to them at angle of approximately 35 degrees from the vertical. This armor upgrading process occurred both on the assembly line and in the field, and brought the protection afforded by the two hatch areas up to approximately the rest of the front area of the hull.

While some M4 series tankers believed that cast hulls were superior in deflecting projectiles to their more box-like welded-hull counterparts, U.S. Army tests between the two types of hulls showed without a doubt that the RHA on the welded-hull M4 series was better at deflecting projectiles. This shows up in a 1950 U.S. Army report titled "The Vulnerability of Armored Vehicles to Ballistic Attack," which came out of the Ordnance Department at Aberdeen Proving Ground, Maryland. It states, "In general, however, the ballistic performance of cast armor is poorer than that of rolled homogeneous armor . . . [which] was found on average 15 percent better in resistance-to-penetration than cast armor. The minimum difference was 6 percent and the maximum was 56 percent."

MORALE BEGINS TO SUFFER

Sergeant Chester J. Marczak sums up the feelings of many M4 series crew members in this quote from a wartime report:

The Germans' high-velocity guns and souped-up ammunition can penetrate our thickest armor. At a range where it would be suicide for us to shoot, they shoot. What we need is more armor, higher velocity, not necessarily a bigger gun, souped-up ammunition, and a means whereby we can maneuver faster, making sharper turns. I've seen many times when the air force was called out to wipe out scattered tanks rather than letting our tanks get slaughtered.

All of us know that the German tanks are far superior to anything that we have in combat. They are able to maneuver on a space the length of their tank. How can we outflank them when all they have to do is pivot and keep their frontal armor toward us? Their frontal armor is practically invulnerable to our 75s, except at an exceptionally close range and they never let us get that close.

We've got a good tank for parades and training purposes but for combat they are just potential coffins. I know! I've left them burning after the first few rounds of German shells penetrated our thickest armor.

As many other M4 series crews in the ETO began losing heart over their odds of survival, morale began to suffer. This led to the attention of American newspaper reporters. Hanson Baldwin wrote the following sentiments in his article printed in the *New York Times* in January 1945: "Why at this late stage in the war are American tanks inferior to the enemy's? That they are inferior the fighting in Normandy showed, and the recent battles in Ardennes have again emphatically demonstrated. This has been denied, explained away and hushed up, but the men who are fighting our tanks against much heavier, better armored and more powerfully armed German monsters know the truth. It is high time that Congress got to the bottom of a situation that does no credit to the War Department. This does not mean that our tanks are bad. They are not; they are good. They are the best tanks in the world—next to the Germans."

In response to mounting criticism in the American press, General George Patton defended the M4 series design in a letter published in the March 31, 1945, issue of *The Army and Navy Journal*:

It has come to my knowledge that certain misguided or perhaps deliberately mendacious individuals, returning from the theater of war, have criticized the equipment of the American soldier. I have been in command of fighting units since the 7th of November 1942, and may therefore claim some knowledge of the various types of equipment. . . . Since 1 August 1944, when the Third Army became operational; our total tank casualties have amounted to 1,136 tanks. During the same period, we have accounted for 2,287 German tanks, of which 808 were of the Tiger or Panther variety, and 851 on our side were M4. These figures of themselves refute any inferiority of our tanks, but let me add that the Third Army has always attacked, and therefore better than 70 percent of our tank casualties have occurred from dug-in antitank guns and not enemy tanks, whereas a majority of the enemy tanks put out have been put out by our tanks. . . . Finally, we must remember that all our tanks have to be transported on steamers and the difference between 40 tons and 70 tons is very marked. The 70-ton tank could never have been brought ashore in landing boats as many of our medium tanks were. Nor could they have marched from the Cotentin Peninsula to the Rhine as practically all of our tanks have been required to do.

Not all U.S. Army generals agreed with Patton's comments. Brigadier General J. H. Collier, commanding Combat Command A of the 2nd Armored Division, stated in a report to General Dwight D. Eisenhower, March 20, 1945: "It is my opinion that press reports of statements by high ranking officers to the effect that we have the best equipment in the world do much to discourage the soldier who is using equipment that he knows to be inferior to that of the enemy. The fact that our equipment must be shipped over long distances does not, in the opinion of our tankers, justify our inferiority. The M4 has proven inferior to the German Mark VI [Tiger] in Africa before the invasion of Sicily, l0 July 1943."

While Patton's confidence in the M4 series tanks may have been justified when looking at the overall big picture of combat in Northwest Europe, for the typical M4 series crew member, it was a much different view. Knowing that German tanks and antitank weapons, hiding in defensive positions, would probably get the first shot in, the tankers had little desire to be the lead tank on any combat operation. They knew that the thin armor on their vehicles offered little or no protection from the enemy's weapons.

On display in Belgium is this second-generation M4A1(76)W. Combat experience with the 76mm gun showed that its standard AP round could only penetrate on average 1 inch more armor than the 75mm AP on first-generation M4 series tanks. *Andreas Kirchoff*

Here is the business end of a 76mm gun mounted on a second-generation M4A3(76)W. Despite the U.S. Army's belief that the 76mm gun would penetrate the thick well-sloped armor on late-war German tanks—like the Panther and the Tiger—combat experience in Northwest Europe quickly demonstrated that this was not the case. *Patton Museum*

CHAPTER FOUR

IMPROVEMENTS

EVEN BEFORE THE M4 SERIES OF TANKS began rolling off the assembly lines in early 1942, the Ordnance Department was considering ways of improving it. By early 1943, the Armored Force concluded that it would have to make do with the M4 series tanks for the rest of the war and set out to modify the vehicle's existing design to improve its combat effectiveness.

Very soon, however, the number of changes requested had grown to such an extent that the need for a major redesign of the entire series became apparent. This effort began in July 1943, and resulted in a much-improved second-generation of M4 series tanks, referred to by the Ordnance Department as the medium tank M4 series (ultimate design). Plans for this series also called for a more powerful 76.2mm gun (referred to as the 76mm gun by the U.S. Army) to be incorporated—then under development by the Ordnance Department. In September 1943, Chrysler received permission to build a number of pilot models of the second-generation M4 series tank that incorporated numerous changes and the latest manufacturing modifications. However, due to delays in acquiring drawings necessary to begin the project, actual work did

not start until December 1943, with the completed and semi-completed second-generation pilots showing up in February 1944.

SECOND-GENERATION MODIFICATIONS

In addition to a new turret and gun mount for the 76mm gun on the second-generation M4 series tanks, another major modification was a new vision commander's cupola, developed by the Libby-Owens-Ford Glass Company. It was fitted with six laminated bullet-resistant glass vision blocks uniformly spaced around a central 21-inch-diameter hatch. There was also a periscope installed in a 360-degree rotating mount in the overhead hatch cover.

Another feature found on some of these tanks was a new suspension system. The new horizontal volute spring suspension (HVSS) system, with wider 23-inch tracks, improved vehicle riding characteristics and off-road flotation.

An important exterior spotting feature seen on second-generation welded-hull versions was a new thicker 47-degree front hull plate (called a glacis), which came with larger, counterbalanced, angled overhead hatches for the driver and assistant driver. This redesign replaced the

An important improvement for the second-generation M4 series tanks was the redesigned tank commander's cupola, seen here from above. It featured six laminated vision blocks. This allowed the tank commander to keep his hatch closed and still observe the terrain around his tank. *Michael Green*

much sharper 56-degree glacis seen on first-generation M4 series tanks. The 56-degree glacis design had also featured very narrow, vertically oriented overhead hatches for the driver and assistant driver and accounted for their hatch protrusions.

With the introduction of the larger hatches for the driver and assistant driver, there also appeared a raised turret bustle in the design. The raised turret bustle's intended purpose was to clear the new larger hatches when the tank's turret pointed in the rearward position, featuring greater clearance under the turret bustle. This made it easier for the driver and assistant driver to leave the vehicle in a hurry without the fear of having the turret block their escape, as often happened on the first-generation M4 series tanks.

One of the most important, though not externally visible, second-generation modifications involved placing of most of the main gun rounds in the tank's hull sub-floor (below the rotating turret basket) in storage racks. The purpose of this redesign was to reduce fires caused by projectiles penetrating the tank's exterior armor and puncturing the metal cartridge cases containing the propellant.

Along with this relocation of the main gun rounds, there were provisions for protecting them by placing liquid-filled metal insert containers, called Ammudamp cans, within the main gun storage racks. The rounds

A close-up picture of the new type of hull overhead hatch found on second-generation M4 series tanks for the driver and assistant driver. The hinge pin was set at a compound angle, which made the new design partially counterbalanced, thus easier to open and close than the earlier design. *Chris Hughes*

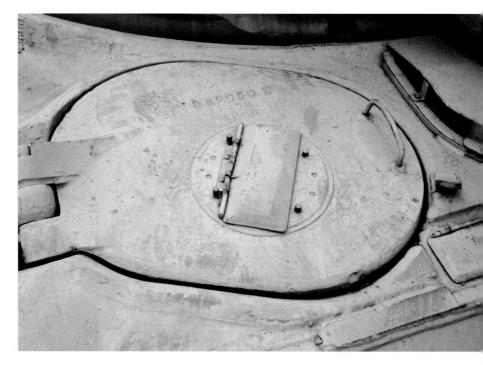

Belonging to the Patton Museum of Cavalry and Armor is this nicely restored M4A3(75)W that often appears in local public events. It is kept spotlessly clean, something not usually seen on its World War II counterparts, except for parade appearances. *Michael Green*

themselves sat in liquid-free cavities that formed part of the storage racks, as the liquid within the metal inserts only engulfed the main gun rounds when penetrated by a projectile. On top of the metal inserts were removable plugs used to refill them if the need arose. Few American tankers seemed to know they were even there or never really paid much attention to them.

Second-generation M4 series tanks equipped with these liquid-filled metal inserts were designated wet stowage (normally shortened to just "W"). The liquid itself consisted of a mixture of water, ethylene glycol to prevent freezing, and a rust inhibitor known as Ammudamp. After wet stowage came into use, tests showed that it actually did not effectively quench the ignition of the propellant charges.

Although the wet stowage system was a failure in service, a suggested replacement of armored containers with higher ammo stowage capacity never materialized.

A 1954 army technical manual on the M4A3 states, "The use of any fluids (water, antifreeze compound, or Ammudamp) in ammunition box cans has been discontinued." All fluids were to be drained, and "those Ammudamp cans that have deteriorated to such an extent that they are no longer suitable for use as separators or barriers for the ammunition" were to be replaced with wood blocks of "the same size and shape as the Ammudamp cans."

UPGRADING THE FIRST-GENERATION M4 SERIES

In late 1943, the Ordnance Department embarked on a remanufacturing program to upgrade the thousands of very early production first-generation M4 series tanks—then employed as training vehicles in the United States. During the rebuilding process, the tanks went through a modernization program, which incorporated the addition of many of the improvements developed after they first rolled off the assembly lines.

Among the technical improvements included were: add-on armor; a modified M34 gun mount with an extension to cover an added direct sight telescope; a spaced-out suspension system to allow fitting of extended end connectors installed on both sides of the tracks; and the new tank commander's second-generation vision cupola. These rebuilt first-generation M4 series tanks then went off to various war zones.

SECOND-GENERATION DESIGNATION CONFUSION

According to an Ordnance Department report, the term "wet" represented not only the fitting of water-protected main-gun ammunition racks, but also indicated that the combat tank so designated had all the other second-generation modifications as well. But the incorporation of the features found on second-generation M4 series tanks were phased in at different times and with different manufacturers over the course of their introduction into the armored force. This meant that many so-called M4 series "wet" tanks did not have all the second-generation features when they rolled off the assembly lines.

This is apparent in the designations of the first batch of second-generation M4 series tanks, all of which were supposedly upgraded with the wet changes, but still lacked installation of the HVSS system—which notably is also missing from their designations. Hence, the M4A1 became the M4A1(76)W, the M4A2 became the M4A2(76)W, and the M4A3 became the M4A3(76)W. The M4 was also slated for the second-generation upgrade program, but the war ended before production began, and with no need for more tanks, the program never got off the drawing board.

SECOND-GENERATION TIMELINE

Upon standardization of second-generation M4 series tanks with the 76mm gun and the wet ammunition storage racks, production of vehicles armed with the 75mm

This official army photograph shows a second-generation M4A3(76)W, which began rolling off the assembly lines in early 1944. Tankers who received the up-gunned second-generation M4 series tanks armed with the 76mm gun were very disappointed to discover that its HE round was inferior to one that fired from the first-generation M4 series tank mounting the 75mm gun. *Patton Museum*

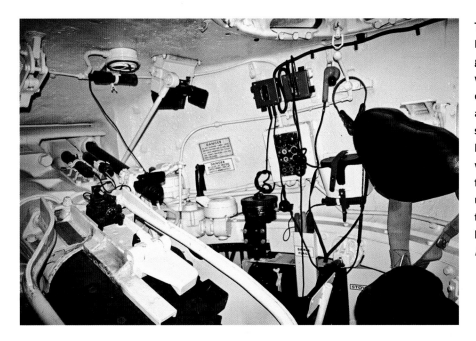

This picture taken from the loader's position on a second-generation M4 series tank armed with a 76mm gun shows the tank commander's two seats. Just above and to the left of the upper seat is the tank commander's hydraulic traverse control handle with a set of headphones hanging from it. The commander could use this control to traverse the turret onto a target before handing it off to the gunner. *Michael Green*

main gun was limited to just the M4A3 tank. These M4A3 tanks, which also had wet ammunition storage racks and other improvements, was designated M4A3(75)W. At this point, those first-generation M4 series tank without the wet storage system came to be called "dry" stowage tanks. For example, the original version of the M4A3 tank was now referred to as the M4A3 (75mm, Dry Stowage).

The first of the second-generation M4 series tanks coming off the assembly lines in January 1944 were the M4A1(76)W variant. They arrived in England in April 1944 for issue to the armored forces, but did not make it to France until the end of July 1944, almost two months after D-day. Pressed Steel Car Company built 3,426 units of the M4A1(76)W by the end of World War II.

Production of the M4A2(76)W began at Fisher Tank Arsenal in May 1944, and continued until the first half of 1945 with 2,894 units completed. The Pressed Steel Car Company also built 21 units of the M4A2(76)W before the war ended. Most of the M4A2(76)W combat tanks were shipped to the Soviet Union as foreign aid.

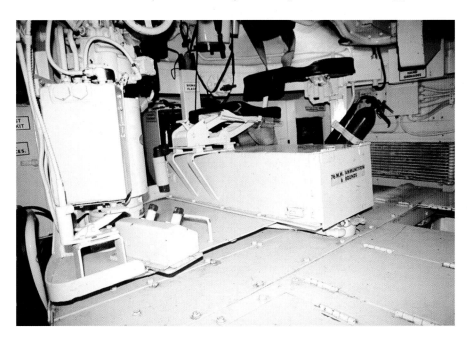

Looking back from the driver's seat on a second-generation M4 series tank armed with a 76mm gun, one can see the vehicle's partial turret basket. The gunner and tank commander's were on a floor, which rotated with the turret, but the loader had to walk around atop the ammo lockers to keep up with turret rotation. In this tank, the main gun is located over the front hull, allowing the loader full access to the 35 main gun rounds in the subfloor. *Michael Green*

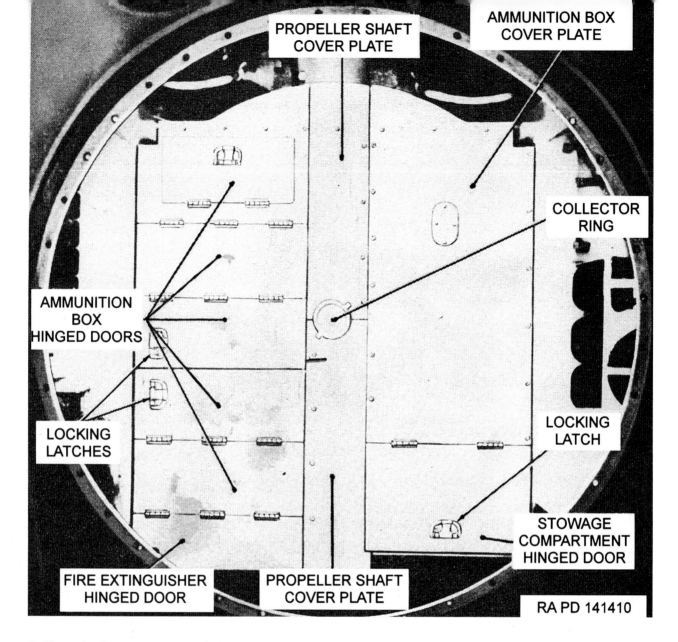

PROPELLER SHAFT
COVER PLATE

AMMUNITION BOX
COVER PLATE

COLLECTOR
RING

AMMUNITION
BOX
HINGED DOORS

LOCKING
LATCHES

LOCKING
LATCH

STOWAGE
COMPARTMENT
HINGED DOOR

FIRE EXTINGUISHER
HINGED DOOR

PROPELLER SHAFT
COVER PLATE

RA PD 141410

An illustration from an army manual shows an overhead view of the subfloor, located under the partial turret basket, of a second-generation M4 series tank armed with a 76mm main gun. Front of the hull is toward the top in this view. At the top of the illustration are the hinged armored doors under which thirty-five main-gun rounds resided.

In February 1944, the Fisher Tank Arsenal began building the first of the M4A3(75)W tanks. Production of this tank would continue until March 1945, with 3,071 units completed. Building of the M4A3(76)W began at Chrysler in March 1944 and ceased in April 1945 with a total of 3,017 units built.

Fisher Tank Arsenal also built 525 units of the M4A3(76)W between September and December 1944. The M4A3, in all its various versions, was the preferred type of M4 series tank in U.S. Army service due to its superior Ford GAA engine powerplant.

A feature not found on the first-generation M4 series tanks, but incorporated on some second-generation versions armed with either the 75mm or 76mm gun, was a tank commander's hydraulic traverse control lever. Mounted on a bracket on the inner turret wall next to the tank commander's position, the control lever enabled the tank commander to override the gunner's turret traverse control handle and to direct the turret via his joystick.

WET AMMUNITION STORAGE DETAILS

With the change to liquid-protected main gun ammunition stowage on second-generation M4 series tanks, a partial turret basket, which occupied only about one-third of the space, replaced the full turret basket. The partial basket permitted access to the main gun ammu-

Looking down from the loader's overhead hatch are the seven angled liquid-filled storage containers (in racks of five), which held thirty-five main-gun rounds with their noses inclined downward. While army manuals called for the rounds to be stored projectile up, those who served on the tanks remember that the rounds were always stored projectile down. *Michael Green*

nition stowed under the subfloor on the loader's side of the tank, but required additional agility on the part of the loader, who now had to walk around on the subfloor to avoid the basket as the turret traversed.

In second-generation M4 series tanks equipped with the 76mm gun and wet storage, the majority of the seventy-one main gun rounds were stored on either side of the driveshaft enclosure under or behind armored hatches. Thirty-five of the main gun rounds sat in vertically angled racks on one side, and thirty sat in horizontal racks on the other side of the interior behind the assistant driver's seat. The remaining six main gun rounds, referred to as ready rounds, resided in an armored box upon which the gunner's seat perched.

A 1949 army manual, on M4A3 tanks armed with the 76mm main gun with the second-generation modifications, describes the order in which the loader withdrew main gun rounds: "The order in which ammunition is withdrawn is based upon the principle of saving the rounds in the ready rack for emergency use. In conformance with this principle, the driver and bow gunner [assistant driver] will pass ammunition to the loader as necessary to assist him in conserving his ready rounds. . . . The most accessible rounds in each section, in addition to the ready rounds are always used last to facilitate rapid reloading in an emergency."

Tom Sator, who eventually became a loader on an M4A3(76)W, remembers that most of the combat actions in which he took part tended to be over very quickly and never required firing more than a half-dozen main-gun rounds. As Tom always had one in the breech, two in his lap and another three on the floor ready to go, he seldom needed to access the main gun storage underneath his feet during an engagement with the enemy.

Not all M4 series tankers were as lucky as Tom in the number of main gun rounds fired in combat. This can be seen in this extract from George Forty's book

Mounted on the floor of the partial turret basket in a second-generation M4 series tank armed with a 76mm gun is this liquid-filled storage container, which stored six main gun rounds and was known as the "ready rack." Army manuals called for loaders to save these rounds for emergency purposes only, as they were the easiest to acquire in the tank. *Michael Green*

Located behind the assistant driver's seat in the second-generation M4 series tank armed with a 76mm gun was a large armored protected storage container that had rack space for thirty main gun rounds. Just in front of the ammunition-storage container was the hull escape hatch. *Michael Green*

titled *Tank Warfare in the Second World War—An Oral History*. The author relates the experience of by Lieutenant Henry J. Earl of the 3rd Armored Division, who commanded an M4 series tank during an all-day battle with German units in November 1944:

> He remembered from experience that if you gave the Germans just 24 hours to dig in, you paid hell getting them out again. And here they'd had almost six weeks to dig in and prepare their defenses. His thoughts were broken by a call from battalion requesting an ammunition report. He called his three remaining tanks for their reports. Then he checked with his loader as to their condition. The

report was: "Just these six rounds on the floor and one in the breech." "My God!" He could vaguely remember firing 40 or 50 rounds, but here they had fired ninety rounds! The reports began to come in. Two tanks had seven rounds each, the other six rounds. He called battalion, giving the report.

With the M4A3(75)W, the main-gun ammunition storage arrangement differed from the M4 series tanks armed with the 76mm gun, since it retained the full turret basket equipped the first-generation M4 series tanks, minus the metal screening. Under the turret basket (in the subfloor) were ten vertically oriented wet ammunition storage racks, containing ten main-gun rounds each. There were another four ready rounds in a wet armored box on the turret basket floor.

For the loader, the only access to the one hundred main-gun rounds stored in the subfloor of the M4A3(75)W came from opening two armored hatches in the bottom of the turret basket floor (located directly under his feet). In prolonged firing of the main gun, this storage arrangement called for turning the tank's turret every so often to allow the loader to access full main-gun-round ammunition storage racks.

HORIZONTAL VOLUTE SPRING SUSPENSION (HVSS) DETAILS

The first-generation M4 series tanks rode on the vertical volute spring suspension (VVSS) system combined with 16 9/16-inch-wide tracks. The shortcomings of this system (inherited from the M3 medium tank) were apparent to all. From the outset, the Ordnance Department looked at other types of suspensions systems as early as December 1941. The system showing the most promise was the HVSS system, first considered for fitting on the M2 medium tank. While the HVSS never appeared on the M2 medium tank, it did make it onto two M3 medium tanks for testing.

In early 1943, the Armored Board began testing two first-generation M4 series tanks fitted with the HVSS system that retained the 16 9/16-inch-wide tracks of the VVSS system. While it showed promise, there was an insufficient degree of improvement to warrant the costly retooling needed to change over the first-generation M4 series tanks from the VVSS system to the new narrow track HVSS system. Work, therefore, began in September 1943 on designing an improved HVSS system that utilized more bogie wheels and wider tracks. Tests proved

This picture shows the arrangement of the vertical storage containers in the hull of an M4A3(75)W with the turret removed. Unlike other versions of the M4A3 tank that allowed access to some of the stored main-gun rounds by the assistant driver, only the loader could access them in the M4A3(75)W. *Bill Nahmens*

this new wider HVSS suspension system was far superior to the narrow track VVSS HVSS systems in durability, flotation, riding qualities, and road wheel life.

By March 1944, the Ordnance Committee recommended the development of the improved HVSS system with 23-inch-wide center-guided tracks for a first-generation M4 pilot vehicle, designated the M4E8. As other M4 series pilot tanks underwent conversion to the new suspension system, their designations also changed. The M4A1 became the M4A1E8, the M4A2 the M4A2E8, and the M4A3 became the M4A3E8.

As the name indicates, the volute springs in the HVSS system were mounted horizontally on the bogie unit instead of vertically. Many elements contributed to the HVSS system's decreased rate of track throwing: elimination of friction from sliding shoes; improved geometric design; addition of shock absorbers (VVSS system equipped M4 series tanks did not have shock

absorbers); rubber-tired bogies; and the use of center-guides instead of outside track guides. The wide track required the use of dual bogies (road wheels), doubling the number of bogie wheels and distributing the wear more uniformly than in the VVSS design.

In early March 1944, the Ordnance Committee recommended HVSS systems to go onto five hundred second-generation M4A3(76)W series tanks. These changes increased the weight of the tanks between 3,000 and 5,000 pounds, depending on the type of track used. It also increased the tank's width to 118 inches with sand shields fitted. On the positive side, the increased width of the new tracks reduced ground pressure from 14.5 psi to about 10 psi. By the end of March 1944, the Ordnance Committee recommended that all second-generation M4 series tanks be fitted with the HVSS system.

In August 1944, the M4A3(76)W started coming off the assembly lines with HVSS suspensions. With the new

M4A3(76)W HVSS

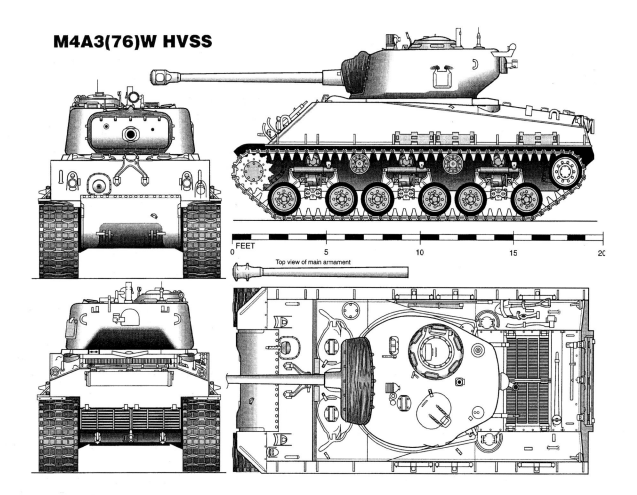

This four-view line drawing shows the various external features of the second-generation M4A3(76)W HVSS tank. The first unit to see combat with the tank proved to be the 4th Armored Division, which received twenty-one of them in late December 1944 and employed them during the Battle of the Bulge. *George Bradford*

suspension system fitted, the tank's designation changed to M4A3(76)W HVSS. The first of these tanks equipped with the HVSS system showed up in Northwest Europe in December 1944.

A mobility comparison test between a captured German Panther tank and an M4A3(76)W HVSS (which is referred to incorrectly as an M4A3E8) conducted by the 2nd Armored Division in early 1945 produced these results: "Operating across typical ground, the Mark V [Panther] left a track imprint one-half inch deep. It did not break through the ground surface. Similar results were obtained with the M4A3E8 [M4A3(76)W HVSS]. Other tanks of the M4 series with narrow track and no track extensions broke through the ground surface, leaving a tank imprint two inches deep."

By the time, the M4A3(76)W HVSS did show up in the ETO, experience had already shown the AGF that a track with the width of 23 or 24 inches was still not wide

enough to keep a tank from bogging down in deep mud. In response, the Ordnance Committee approved production of kits for field installation of 39-inch grousers for this tank model. These were still in development for the M4A3(76)W HVSS when World War II ended; therefore it never went in production.

The M4A1(76)W and the M4A2(76)W also got the HVSS system before their production ceased. Like the M4A3(76)W, their designations had "HVSS" added to indicate that they were not equipped with the earlier VVSS system. M4 series tank authority Joe DeMarco has uncovered written documentation that shows the American First and Third Army received an allotment of M4A1(76)W HVSS tanks starting on April 6, 1945. Efforts by many Sherman tank history buffs have yet to uncover any pictorial evidence showing them in troop service before the war in the ETO officially ended in May 1945. Pictorial evidence, however, does show that the

Patton Museum volunteers dressed in period uniforms are awaiting the go-ahead to operate this M4A3(76)W HVSS during a public demonstration. Notice the external travel lock on the front upper hull plate and the siren mounted next to the driver's side headlight. *Kathy Brown*

Red Army used the M4A2(76)W HVSS in combat against the Japanese Army in Manchuria in June 1945.

Various versions of the M4 tank series equipped with the 76mm main gun and HVSS system appeared in U.S. National Guard and Reserve service after World War II. The M4A2(76)W HVSS showed up in Canadian Army service after World War II.

SECOND-GENERATION ASSAULT TANK

Even before the Normandy landings, the U.S. Army anticipated that as Allied forces pushed out of France and into the German homeland, they would encounter increasingly organized and fortified German defensive positions. Therefore, they needed a tank with both a heavier gun and thicker armor to attack these prepared positions. The army had hoped that the M26 Pershing heavy tank, armed with a 90mm main gun, would be available by late 1944. But as this was not the case, a decision materialized to use a drastically up-armored M4A3(75)W tank in the assault role. An agreement to manufacture 254 such tanks quickly appeared, and the Ordnance Committee designated the tank as the M4A3E2 in March 1944. The "E2" part of the designation indicated it was an experimental design only.

Construction of the M4A3E2 proceeded rapidly and the first units entered into combat in the ETO in late

On display in front of the Patton Museum of Cavalry and Armor, located at Fort Knox, Kentucky, is a second-generation M4A3(76)W with the wide track HVVS system. It proved to be a vast improvement over the narrow first-generation M4 series VVSS system. *Michael Green*

Belonging to a private collector is an M4A1(76)W HVSS on display during a military collectors' rally. Military records show that a number of them made it to Northwest Europe during the closing weeks of the war in Europe, but did not see combat. *Michael Green*

1944. American tankers greeted their arrival with great enthusiasm because they appreciated the extra protection they received from the tank's extra-thick armor protection levels and quickly asked for more of them. In the field, the M4A3E2 tank was nicknamed the "Jumbo."

Power for the Jumbo came from the standard Ford V-8 GAA tank engine and the final-drive gear ratio was changed to compensate for the increased weight and to provide for maximum speed of 22 miles per hour.

The normal role for the Jumbo was that of point tank (leading a column), as it could absorb the projectiles fired from German tank and antitank guns that would have left standard M4 series tanks burning piles of wreckage.

The distinguishing features of the Jumbo included a new final-drive casting, interchangeable with that of the

standard production tank. The front nose of the casting was 5.5 inches thick, with 4.5 inches on its sloping surfaces. A 1.5-inch-thick piece of armor went on to the glacis of the tank, giving it a total frontal hull thickness of 4 inches.

A new turret with 6 inches of armor sat on top of the hull of the Jumbo. The frontal rotor shield provided 7 inches of armor protection to the 75mm gun mount. Rolled armor, 1.5 inches thick, appeared on the upper side plates of the hull of the Jumbo. There was no additional armor on the side plates below the upper hull level or on the rear of the tank.

The Jumbo rode on the VVSS system. Due to the vehicle's increased weight, roughly up to 42 tons, extended end connectors were fitted on the outside of the track

Parked side-by-side in this photograph are two different versions of the M4 series tanks belonging to a private collector. The tank on the right is a first-generation M4A3 (dry storage) armed with a 75mm main gun and fitted with a second-generation tank commander's vision cupola. It rides on the VVSS system. The tank on the left is an M4A1(76)W HVSS. *Michael Green*

strands to maintain a ground pressure of about 14 psi. Normal ground pressure for most M4 series tanks ranged from 13.2 to 14.4 psi.

There was a price to pay for all that extra armor on the Jumbo, as seen in this army report dated October 24, 1944: "One thing that users must realize is that in rough cross-country operation the front volute springs will fail if permitted to 'bottom' violently."

Although the original intent was to mount a 76mm gun, the Jumbo tank received the standard 75mm M3 gun since it fired a better HE round. The Jumbo came with enough internal room to stow 106 main gun rounds in wet storage containers. The Jumbo also mounted the same secondary armament found on other M4 series tanks, which included two .30-caliber guns and one .50-caliber machine gun. During deployment in Northwest Europe, some Jumbos had their 75mm guns replaced with the 76mm gun.

With only 254 Jumbos built, the demand quickly outstripped available supply in Northwest Europe. To placate the demand, in early 1945 General George S. Patton, commander of the Third Army, ordered that M4A3(76)W and M4A3(76)W HVSS tanks in his command "not already equipped with heavy armor plate similar to that on the M4A3E2 were to be modified with the least practicable delay."

As a result of Patton's order, many disabled welded-hull M4 series tanks had their front glacis plates and upper side hull armor cut off with acetylene torches and welded onto operational versions of the M4A3(76)W and M4A3(76)W HVSS tanks in his command. The armor from captured German tanks was also used in this up-armoring effort.

The Third Army's up-armoring program took place under contract with local civilian firms located in its area of operation. Within a span of three weeks, it is estimated that about one hundred operational M4A3(76)W and M4A3(76)W HVSS combat tanks went through the up-armoring process ordered by Patton. The Third Army also received a number of knocked-out M4 series tanks from the Seventh Army for converting into what some now refer to as "Expedient Jumbos."

With the conclusion of the war in the ETO in May 1945, many of the remaining Jumbos were shipped back to the United States in anticipation of them taking part in the planned invasion of Japan, which fortunately never took place.

According to well-versed M4 series tank authority Joe DeMarco, ninety-six Jumbos remained listed in the army's inventory as of August 1948. Of that number, three received the HVSS system and new flamethrower turrets between 1947 and 1948. Pictorial evidence indicates that at least a few Jumbos were still in service with the Minnesota National Guard as late as 1955.

SECOND-GENERATION HOWITZER ARMED TANKS

One of the original characteristics of the first-generation M4 series tanks was the removable front plate of the turret constituting the gun mount, which could accommodate any one of five different combinations of weapons. One of the suggested combinations was a 105mm howitzer with a .30-caliber coaxial machine gun. Work on standardizing this configuration began in early 1942, shortly after the first-generation M4 series tank armed with the 75mm gun went into production.

Although equipped with the same weapon as the direct-support artillery battalions, the howitzer-armed M4 series tanks were not intended as a substitute for artillery. Their mounts did not allow for the high angles of fire associated with artillery, and the organizations into which they were assigned did not have the fire direction and meteorological capability of dedicated

On display at a U.S Army museum is this rare example of an M4A3E2 tank, nicknamed the "Jumbo." This version of the tank featured a dramatic increase in armor protection over the standard M4A3(75)W, with 7 inches of armor on the front of the turret and 4 inches on the front hull plate. The cast differential was 5 1/2 inches at its thickest portion. *Dan Reed*

Pictured being refueled in the ETO is a M4A3(76)W HVSS tank with an elaborate metal mounting cage on both its turret and hull filled with sandbags. While sandbags provided little in the way of protection from German AP projectiles, they did have some success in defeating German shaped-charge warheads fired from the Panzerschrecks and Panzerfausts. *Patton Museum*

artillery units. Rather, the howitzers were intended to furnish a large-capacity HE shell to reduce heavily fortified positions. The proven 105mm howitzer system already had an existing support structure of training, maintenance, and ammunition supply, so it offered a ready solution to the impending problem of how to deal with fortified positions.

A howitzer is a comparatively short cannon with a medium muzzle velocity and a curved trajectory that is between the cannon and the mortar. The higher, curving trajectory allows this weapon's projectiles to reach targets generally hidden and not easily engaged by flat trajectory guns. Guns, as compared with howitzers, have a longer barrel, higher muzzle velocity, and flatter projectile trajectory.

In November 1942, two first-generation M4A4s were modified for installation of the M2A1 105mm howitzer and were designated M4A4E1 by Ordnance Committee action in December 1942. The mount itself was designated T70. Necessary modifications to the tank included substitution of 105mm ammunition containers in place of the smaller racks, installation of gyrostabilizer equipment designed for the 105mm howitzer mount, and minor changes in internal stowage. There was stowage space in the M4A4E1 for fifty-eight rounds of 105mm ammunition.

One of the howitzer-armed pilot vehicles went to Aberdeen Proving Ground, and the other went to the Armored Force Board. Tests at Aberdeen showed that the 105mm howitzer mounted in the first-generation

The crews of cast hull M4 series tanks also attached extra armor plates to their vehicles, as this picture seems to indicate. The vehicle pictured is second-generation M4A1(76)W fitted with a flat armor plate against the rounded front hull contours of the tank. *Patton Museum*

M4 series turret proved awkward for the crew to both load and fire. The turret was also badly unbalanced, so much so that the power traverse system would not work properly if the vehicle sat on a side slope of more than 30 degrees. As a result of this test program a number of features were redesigned, ultimately leading to considerable savings in weight and interior space for the vehicle.

During a conference held at Fort Knox, Kentucky, in February 1943, the many new modifications to the proposed 105mm howitzer-armed version received approval for further development. Other decisions included the use of a partial turret basket, omission of the power traverse and gyrostabilizer, allowance for a partial recoil guard for the howitzer, and a redesign of the interior to stow more 105mm howitzer ammunition. The increased ammunition load would be a mix of HE and WP, with a few HEAT rounds for good measure.

Two pilot models with a modified 105mm howitzer installation soon appeared and received the designation M4E5. Testing of the pilot models proved satisfactory, and the Armored Board concluded that the M4E5 was ready for fielding after the inclusion of a ventilating fan and an improved T93 direct-sight telescope into the turret.

The production versions of the M4E5 were built on second-generation M4 or M4A3 tanks built by Chrysler, minus the wet stowage system. Approximately 4,680

came off the assembly lines between February 1944 and June 1945. Most rode on the HVSS system, but those that saw service during World War II rode into combat on the VVSS system. The designations for the vehicles included the M4(105), the M4(105) HVSS, M4A3(105), and M4A3(105) HVSS.

The second-generation M4 and M4A3 tanks armed with the 105mm howitzer replaced the open-topped M7 self-propelled howitzer, also armed with a 105mm howitzer. Each tank battalion featured six of the 105mm armed M4 series howitzer tanks—three in the Headquarters Company and one in each of the three medium tank companies. They provided indirect-fire support with HE to the various platoons and companies of the battalion and could supply a smoke screen at short notice with the WP round.

Although the M7s had proved successful in replacing their towed 105mm predecessors in field artillery battalions, their lack of overhead armor protection limited their suitability to accompany tanks in the close combat role. While artillery battalions usually fought from beyond enemy mortar and small arms range, the M7s were vulnerable in close combat. Therefore, the howitzer-armed M4 series tanks were well received in the tank battalions.

After World War II, the Marine Corps disposed of most of its first-generation M4A2 and M4A3 tanks, keeping only the M4A3(105) HVSS in service. It would later go on to see service in the Korean War as an infantry support weapon. The M4A3(105) HVSS disappeared from Marine Corps service by the end of the 1950s.

THE STORY BEHIND THE 76MM GUN

Predating the development of the second-generation M4 series tank was the Ordnance Department's attempt at up-gunning the first-generation M4 series tank, beginning in late 1941. At the time, the Ordnance Department wanted a gun with the penetrating ability of the M7 3-inch gun standardized for arming the M6 heavy tank (that never went into production). Unfortunately, the M7 gun was too heavy for the existing M4 series turret and M34 gun mount, so development began on the lighter T1 76mm gun.

To avoid the huge effort involved in developing, producing, and supplying new ammunition for the T1 76mm gun, the Ordnance Department decided to use the projectiles (AP, HE, WP) already designed for the M7 3-inch gun—which, despite its different nomenclature, actually had the same bore diameter as the 76mm gun. The 3-inch rounds were attached to a smaller diameter metal cartridge case, which contained a less powerful propellant charge but still retained the same muzzle

Lacking enough M4A3E2 Jumbo tanks in the Third Army, its commander, General George S. Patton, quietly ordered that all M4A3(76)W HVSS be up-armored with the cut-out armor of knocked-out American and German tanks. The vehicle pictured seems to have armor from a cut-up Tiger tank welded to both sides of its turret and at least one hull side. Additional plates are welded or bolted over the glacis. *Tank Museum*

velocity of 2,600 feet per second as the M7. Even better, as far as the Ordnance Department was concerned, was the fact that the T1 retained the same breech ring as the M3 75mm gun already mounted in the M4 series tanks, making the conversion easier.

Ammunition nomenclature is often assigned arbitrarily to denote different cartridges, even those containing the same projectile. These name differences solve the problem of similar-sounding ammunition items being ordered by units with two different types of tank gun. Even though the 3-inch gun on the M10 tank destroyer and the 76mm on the second-generation M4 series tanks had the same bore diameter, the cartridges were not interchangeable.

Two of the newly built 76mm guns T1 were tested at Aberdeen Proving Ground, Maryland, in August 1942. One of the guns went onto a fixed test stand, and the other into the turret of an M4A1 series tank. Due to the extreme length of the T1 barrel, the tank's turret proved to be badly unbalanced in operation. To correct this unforeseen problem, 15 inches of the T1 gun barrel was removed, and weight was added to the weapon's breech ring.

Pleased with the results of T1 firing tests, the Ordnance Department recommended that M4 series tanks be armed with the now-standardized 76mm gun M1. The shortened version of the T1 became the 76mm gun M1A1.

The following quote is from an Ordnance Department report concerning an up-gunned M4 series tank now designated as the M4A1 (76M1): "Because of the greatly increased firepower available, the Ordnance Committee stated that the tank equipment with the 76mm gun should be placed in production as soon as practicable, but that it should be classified as Substitute Standard until the application had been thoroughly proved and necessary refinements in design had been made."

BACK TO THE DRAWING BOARD

At the time, the Ordnance Department envisioned that a production order for at least 1,000 units of the M4 series armed with the new 76mm gun M1 would soon appear. However, Armored Force testing of additional examples of the up-gunned M4A1 tanks (conducted between February 1943 and April 1943) led it to believe that the turret arrangement (as recommended by the Ordnance Committee) was unsatisfactory, mainly because of inadequate turret space.

Since General Jacob Devers, who commanded the Armored Forces, strongly believed in the need for a

Taking part in the Patton Museum of Cavalry and Armor's annual 4th of July living history show is this nicely restored M4A3(105) equipped with the VVSS system. The rotor shield on the 105mm howitzer-armed version differed slightly from the one on the standard 75mm main-gun-armed tank. The former had four large bolts arranged around the point at which the barrel projected out from the rotor shield. *Chun Lun Hsu*

76mm main gun on the M4 series tank, in May 1943 the Ordnance Committee recommended the development of two new, improved pilot tanks. Designated the M4E6, these pilot tanks incorporated a number of changes desired by the Armored Force.

Rather than take the time to design a new turret with space for a larger main gun, the Ordnance Department decided to graft onto the M4E6 hull the preproduction version of a cast-armor turret, originally developed for the T23 medium tank (a part of the T20 series of tanks). The main armament consisted of the 76mm gun M1A1 and not the 76mm gun M1, since Ordnance Department testing had showed the 76mm gun M1 to be defective.

BETTER LUCK THE SECOND TIME AROUND

Of the two M4E6 tanks built and delivered by Chrysler in July 1943, one remained at the Detroit Tank Arsenal while the other went to Aberdeen Proving Ground for testing by the Ordnance Department. After that, it went to Fort Knox, Kentucky, for testing by the Armored Force. After the Armored Force Board obtained positive results during test firing, it drafted a letter dated August 17, 1943, that recommended the acceptance and immediate production of up-gunned M4 series tanks based on the M4E6 design. The first to enter into production was the M4A1(76)W in January 1944.

A relatively new addition to the Patton Museum of Cavalry and Armor is this slightly worse-for-wear M4A3(105) HVSS found in Iraq by the U.S. Army. An external spotting feature for the howitzer-armed version was the slightly shorter and thicker barrel compared to the standard 75mm-gun-armed version. *Michael Green*

At the same time, the Chief of Ordnance received instructions to discontinue production of 75mm main-gun-equipped tanks from the AGF Headquarters. However, the Armored Force indicated that it did not want to completely drop the 75mm main gun from production. It pointed out that the HE projectile for the 75mm main gun was far superior to the one for the 76mm main gun. Somebody must have also pointed out that the Marine Corps and the British Army (plus its Commonwealth allies) still needed the M4 series tank armed with the 75mm gun.

One of the biggest problems with the 76mm tank guns fitted to the M4 series was the weapon's muzzle blast and the resulting target obscuration from smoke and dust. To correct this problem, the Ordnance Department came up with a two-part solution: a longer primer

in the round's cartridge case that improved the burning rate of the propellant, and a redesigned muzzle brake to be fitted to the 76mm gun M1A1.

Those equipped with the threaded barrels for the fitting of a muzzle brake became the 76mm gun M1A1C, while a later model having rifling with a tighter twist became the 76mm gun M1A2. The tighter rifling improved projectile stability in flight, which in turn produced a slight increase in penetration at longer ranges. When no muzzle brake was available for fitting on threaded 76mm guns, a protective ring was installed to guard the threads from damage.

Major Paul A. Bane Jr., of the 2nd Armored Division, discusses tank muzzle brakes in a wartime report: "Our tank crews operating tanks equipped with 76mm guns have experienced great difficulty observing the

Belonging to a private collector is this 105mm howitzer motor carriage M7, which is nicknamed the "Priest" for its pulpit-like machine gun station on the right front of the vehicle. Operating alongside M4 series tanks was a dicey proposition due to its open-topped design, covered with a foul-weather tarp, as seen on the vehicle pictured. Its shortcomings led to the fielding of the M4 series tanks armed with a 105mm howitzer. *Michael Green*

strike of a round due to excessive muzzle blast. It was necessary to use dismounted observers. Recently we have received a few M4A3E8 [M4A3(76)W HVSS] tanks equipped with muzzle brakes. Test firing and combat operations have proven the muzzle brake to be a great help. We consider muzzle brakes an essential part of the tank gun."

THE 76MM MAIN GUN ROUNDS

Besides the M88 smoke round, the up-gunned second-generation M4 series tanks with the 76mm main gun fired a 22-pound HE round, designated the M42A1. The projectile portion of the round weighed approximately 12 pounds and left the muzzle of the gun tube at 2,700 feet per second.

The standard AP round for the up-gunned second-generation M4 series tanks with the 76mm main gun was

the 24-pound M62 APC-T. The projectile portion of the round weighed about 15 pounds and attained a muzzle velocity of 2,600 feet per second. It could penetrate about 1-inch-thicker armor than the APC-T projectile fired from the 75mm main gun, which had a muzzle velocity of only 2,030 feet per second. Late production examples of the M62 APC-T round came with a HE filler and a base detonating fuse, earning it the designation M62 APC-HE-T.

There was also another AP round for the 76mm tank gun designated the M79 Shot AP-T. The complete round weighed 24 pounds. While the 15-pound projectile featured the same muzzle velocity of an M61 APC-T, the lack of a ballistic cap affected its armor penetration performance at longer ranges.

In the field, the M62 APC-T round's performance proved a disappointment to many. Second Lieutenant

The original 76mm gun T1 in this picture is mounted on a very early production M4A1. Due to its extreme length, the turret on this example of the M4A1 tank proved badly out of balance. Fifteen inches came off of the muzzle end of the barrel to help solve this problem. *Patton Museum*

Frank Seydel Jr., of the 2nd Armored Division, describes the round when it was used in a combat action in a wartime report: "On March 3rd at Bosinghoven, I took under fire two German Mark V [Panther] tanks at a range of 600 yards. At this time, I was using a 76mm gun, using APC for my first round. I saw this round make a direct hit on a vehicle and ricochet into the air. I fired again at a range of 500 yards and again observed a direct hit, after which I threw about 10 rounds of mixed APC and HE, leaving the German tank burning."

When the news regarding the poor penetration performance of the 76mm main gun and its standard AP rounds reached General Dwight D. Eisenhower (supreme Allied commander), he said in a conversation with General Omar Bradley, "You mean our 76 won't knock these Panthers out? I thought it was going to be the wonder gun of the war." Bradley answered, "Oh it's better than the 75, but the new charge [propellant] is much too small. She just hasn't the kick to carry her through the German armor." Eisenhower answered Bradley's comment by stating, "Why is it that I am always the last to hear about this stuff? Ordnance told me this 76 would take care of anything the Germans had. Now I find you can't knock out a damn thing with it."

In an effort to perfect mounting a cut-down 76mm gun T1 (now designated as the M1) in the turret, the Ordnance Department had twelve later-production M4A1 tanks built with a modified turret, which had a counterweight fitted as a turret bustle, as shown in this picture. In this configuration the tank was designated the M4A1(76M1). *Patton Museum*

With the rejection of the M4A1(76M1) concept by the U.S. Army Armored Force, the Ordnance Department attempted to come up with something that it would find acceptable. That tank was the M4E6 pilot, pictured here. It featured the turret and gun mount developed for another medium tank design with the addition of a 76mm main gun on a second-generation M4 hull. *Patton Museum*

M4 series tank authority Joe DeMarco discovered in his research at the National Archives a surprising bit of information regarding the 13th Tank Battalion, which formed part of the 1st Armored Division in Northwest Europe between August 3, 1944, and December 31, 1944. During that time, the unit's M4 series tanks armed with the 76mm main guns expended 19,634 rounds of HE and only 55 rounds of M62 APC-T.

WHO WAS AT FAULT?

The 76mm tank gun's inability to punch through the frontal armor of German tanks was the fault of the Ordnance Department. It failed to correctly assess the technical capabilities of German armor plate, and this led to the deployment of a 76mm tank gun that could not fulfill its intended role.

The Ordnance Department received a great deal of information on both the Tiger and Panther, yet it failed to properly evaluate it. Thus the penetration ability of American tank guns (like the 76mm) against enemy armor plate was overestimated and the quality of German armor plate and its manner of construction underrated and discounted.

As an example, throughout the war the Ordnance Department tested the effectiveness of its tank guns and ammunition against nearly vertical plates of steel armor, which did not match the configuration or profile of any German tank. While the Ordnance Department did try to account for the increased effectiveness of sloping armor plate by using mathematical calculations, it failed to take into account the tendency of tank rounds to bounce (or ricochet) off from angled armor plate.

In September 1943, Major General Alvan C. Gillem (Armored Force commander) wrote a letter to General Lesley J. McNair (AGF commander) stating that based on figures provided by the Ordnance Department, the 76mm tank gun could penetrate the frontal armor of a German Tiger tank at a range of 2,000 yards. This figure later proved incredibly optimistic, since combat in Europe showed that the 76mm tank gun could only penetrate the Tiger's frontal armor at less than 50 yards.

The Ordnance Department's optimistic assessment of the 76mm gun was enthusiastically accepted without further testing or analysis. The U.S. Army remained convinced of its validity until its tanks began battling the German tanks in Normandy, France, in the summer of 1944. This assessment contributed to the unwillingness of the Ordnance Department to field any tank destroyers with a gun bigger than the 76mm.

IMPROVED TANK AMMUNITION

To increase the penetrating ability of the 76mm gun, the Ordnance Department developed a new main gun round designated the M93 hypervelocity armor piercing (HVAP) solid shot. It was nicknamed "Hyper-Shot" by the tank crews.

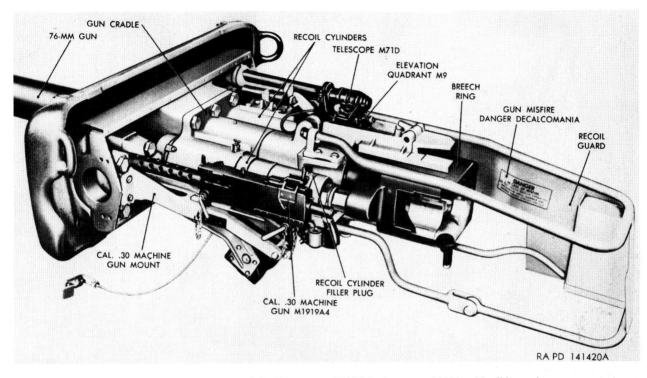

RA PD 141420A

From an army manual comes this illustration of the 76mm gun M1A2 in gun mount M62, with all its various components listed. Total weight of the gun and gun mount was 3,206 pounds.

While the complete HVAP round weighed 18.9 pounds, the lightweight 9.4-pound projectile consisted of a dense core of tungsten carbide with an aluminum outer body, nose, and windshield. There was a tracer element in the base of the projectile initiated by the propelling charge upon firing.

With a muzzle velocity of 3,400 feet per second, the projectile portion of the M93 HVAP could penetrate 6.2 inches of armor at 500 yards (almost double that of the M62 APC-T main gun round). It was supposed to penetrate up to 5.3 inches of armor at 1,000 yards. At 1,500 yards, penetration was 4.6 inches of armor, and at 2,000 yards it was 3.9 inches of armor.

As soon as the first M93 HVAP rounds came off the production line, they were transported by air to Northwest Europe around August 1944, and then to the tankers in the field. Each 76mm-gun-armed M4 series tank was supposed to have a moderate supply of this special ammunition.

Major Paul A. Bane Jr., of the 2nd Armored Division, comments in a wartime report, "Our tank crews have had some success with the HVAP 76mm ammunition. However, at no time have we been able to secure more than five rounds per tank and in recent actions this has been reduced to a maximum of two rounds, and in many tanks all this type has been expended without being replaced."

Sergeant Ross Figueroa, of the 2nd Armored Division, is quoted in a wartime report discussing the merits of HVAP: "We have found that the HVAP does not bounce off the enemy tanks like the APC. . . . I honestly believe that we should have much more of the ammo than is now being issued. The few rounds (4) we now have are hardly sufficient, should we ever encounter enemy armor in numbers. The HVAP ammo has proved beyond a doubt its value, especially when I know it will penetrate enemy armor at 1,600 yards or more. I feel that we should have more of the high-velocity ammo and if possible half of our basic load should be of that type."

An April 27, 1945, letter to the Office of the army's Surgeon General from Colonel Willard Machle and Lieutenant General Frederick S. Brackett, who went to observe problems in tank units in Northwest Europe, states: "HVAP has not been available in sufficient quantity to have any significant influence. Tankers' grab for it as a drowning man for a straw, though few regard it as adequate."

The HVAP round was a big improvement over the standard M62 APC-T main gun round, but it did not

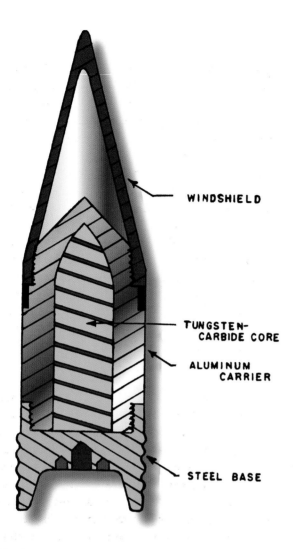

WINDSHIELD

TUNGSTEN-CARBIDE CORE

ALUMINUM CARRIER

STEEL BASE

The hypervelocity armor-piercing (HVAP) projectile consists of an extremely hard tungsten carbide core held within an outer aluminum carrier with an attached windshield to improve its in-flight performance. Crew often referred to this ammunition as "Hyper-Shot" to distinguish it from the older APC design. *James D. Brown*

always do the job. First Lieutenant William L. Schaubel, of the 2nd Armored Division, describes in a wartime report a combat encounter with Tiger tanks in which he used HVAP: "At Oberemot, Germany, 27 February 1945, our second platoon on road block was engaged by two Tiger tanks, Mark VI, at 3,600 yards, and two of our Shermans were knocked out. Our 3,400 feet per second 76mm HVAP ammunition was used and bounced off the side slopes, seven rounds. Definitely outranged due to better sights in the Mark VI and more muzzle velocity in their souped-up ammunition. Upon throwing smoke at the Tiger tanks, they withdrew because smoke means marking target for artillery and fighter-bombers to the Germans."

GETTING SOMEBODY INTERESTED IN THE 76MM

Prior to the invasion of France in June 1944, a number of demonstrations of the new 76mm-gun-armed M4 series tanks occurred in England for senior U.S. Army officers. Everyone who saw the firepower demonstrations came away impressed. Yet, most high-level armor commanders decided that they would rather stick with the familiar 75mm gun on the M4 series than retrain their troops to use a new gun.

Even General George S. Patton, who witnessed a demonstration of 76mm-gun-armed M4 series tanks six days after D-day, decided he would take the new gun only if first placed into separate tank battalions for a combat test.

Patton changed his tune after the Battle of the Bulge, which ran from December 1944 through January 1945, when his Third Army made plans to make up for the shortage of second-generation 76mm-gun-armed M4 series tanks by mounting 76mm guns in first-generation M4 series tanks. Pictorial evidence indicates some of these vehicles saw combat at the end of the war in the ETO with the Third Army.

This lack of interest in a bigger, and supposedly better, gun for the M4 series seems strange for those who look back in hindsight. At the time, though, the AGF still had complete faith in the 75mm-gun-armed M4 series tanks. Combat in North Africa (in early 1942) and fighting in Sicily and Italy (beginning in the summer of 1943) had shown that the M4 series tanks with the 75mm gun compared well with older model German tanks of the time.

While a small number of German Tiger I tanks saw action in North Africa, Sicily and later in Italy, poor tactics and even worse terrain limited their effectiveness, giving American tankers a false sense of security. The German Panther tank saw limited action in Italy, but also failed to generate any doubts within the AGF about the ability of the 75mm-gun-armed M4 series tanks to outperform the enemy.

Part of the problem lay with the arrogance of the AGF, which did not believe in the development of any weapon that it did not consider essential, despite how much the troops in the field wanted or needed it. In contrast, the Ordnance Department believed in maintaining a strong lead over the user arms (the AGF, the Armored Force, and the Armored Force Board) in the development of new equipment. This attitude came from the

This close-up picture shows a British Army M4 tank (a late-production composite hull variant) armed with the 17-pounder, the only tank gun during the fighting in the ETO in 1944 and most of 1945 that had a chance of penetrating the frontal armor of late-war German tanks. *Patton Museum*

fact that Ordnance officers were devoted to the study of overall weapons effectiveness, whereas the line officers in the AGF were only concerned with tactical performance.

As events transpired during World War II, the Ordnance Department proved correct in its perception of the inadequacies of M4 armament and armor protection. Having pushed for a heavy tank, with little result, since 1942, the Ordnance Department suffered a great deal of criticism by the AGF as late as 1943. Within less than two years, in January 1945, the Ordnance Department would find itself criticized by the AGF for just the opposite reason—not having fielded a well-armed heavy tank by then. Whatever response the Ordnance Department leadership had to the AGF with regard to this criticism is lost to history.

OPPORTUNITY MISSED

The most unfortunate aspect of the planning for up-gunning of the M4 series with the 76mm gun is the fact that the army had the opportunity to mount a 90mm gun in the M4 series tanks as early as 1943. The Office of the Chief of Military History, in its published work on the technical services in World War II, mentions the aborted development of a 90mm-armed M4 series tank:

An attempt by the Armored Force Board in the fall of 1943 to provide the M4 with a more powerful

gun, the 90mm, had failed. Ordnance had begun development work on the 90mm antiaircraft gun to adapt it for use on tanks and gun motor carriages [tank destroyers] early in the war, after reports from Cairo [Egypt] had indicated that the Germans in Libya [North Africa] were successfully using their 88mm gun against tanks, and the new antitank 90mm was standardized as the M3 in September 1943. Thereupon, the Armored Force Board, believing that the M4 Sherman tank was the one tank that could be delivered in time for the invasion of Europe, recommended that the 90mm gun be installed on a thousand M4A3 tanks. Major General Gladeon M. Barnes, chief of the Ordnance Department's Research and Development Service, refused to go along with the recommendation; and General McNair turned it down on the advice of his G-3 Brigadier General John M. Lentz.

General Barnes had nothing against the 90mm gun. On the contrary, he and others had done everything they could to get it mounted on a tank destroyer, against the heated objections of the AGF, which continued to insist that 75mm and 76mm guns on the M4 series tanks were adequate. Thanks largely to General Barnes' efforts, supported by the Tank Destroyer Board, the M36 tank destroyer armed with a 90mm got to the ETO in late 1944. Strangely enough, General Barnes did not want the 90mm gun mounted in the M4 series of tanks. He felt very strongly that the gun was too heavy for the tank and believed that it would have produced "too much of an unbalanced design." General Barnes was of the strong belief that American tanks should not be fighting German tanks, which was the job of specialized tank destroyers.

After the Allied invasion of Europe, the army quickly became aware of the limitations of the 76mm gun firing its standard AP ammunition. At that point in the war, everybody wanted better-armed tanks. General Omar Bradley noted that the 76mm gun often "scuffed rather than penetrated" the heavy armor of the Panthers and Tigers.

In July 1944, General Eisenhower sent General Joseph A. Holly (his staff armored officer) back to the United States to encourage the shipment to Northwest Europe of additional M36 tank destroyers. While in Detroit, Holly had the opportunity to see an M4(105) VVSS chassis, modified by Chrysler, mounting an M26 Pershing tank turret armed with a 90mm main gun. In a July 25, 1944, letter from Holly to a fellow officer, he

The crew members of this U.S. Army M4A3(76)W HVSS are firing their turret-mounted M2 .50-caliber machine gun at enemy positions during the Korean War. The first of these tanks showed up in South Korea on July 31, 1950, and entered into combat two days later. *Patton Museum*

discusses the progress on the M26 Pershing heavy tank and his opinion of the up-gunned M4 series tank fitted with the Pershing turret:

There was a second possibility of getting a 90mm Gun Tank that was to modify the M4 Medium Tank. In Detroit I saw a job that had been modified by Chrysler Engineering; it was not a bad effort. All factors considered, had we been able to get immediate deliveries, it would have presented tempting possibilities. It was estimated, however, that deliveries could not be made prior to January [1945], and any cobbling progress would interfere with the production of the T26. There was no net gain in selecting the cobbled M4. The decision was made not to proceed with any cobbling of M4, and to devote all facilities available towards furthering T26 production.

Many American tankers tended to believe that no matter what the Ordnance Department did, the M26 Pershing tank would never have made it to Europe in time to be of any real value during the war. Instead, many believed that if the M4 series of tanks had received a 90mm gun in 1943 (if only as a backup for the M26 Pershing's failure to get into combat in late 1944), it would have provided enough firepower in Northwest Europe to save the lives of many tankers—those killed or maimed because their vehicles failed to mount main guns with sufficient penetration abilities to deal with late war German tanks.

THE 17-POUNDER OPTION

The British Army began to think about putting bigger, more powerful tank guns in their vehicles in early 1941. However, the appearance of the German Panther tank in Italy in the summer of 1943 provided the catalyst for the British Army to mount its 76.2mm towed antitank gun—called the 17-pounder—into a suitable tank turret. That tank turret turned out to be from the first-generation M4 series.

The 17-pounder gun fitted in the M4 series turret was roughly equivalent to the German Panther tank's 75mm gun. It was also slightly superior in penetrating the armor plate to both the early model German 88mm guns (like one found on the Tiger I) and the 90mm tank gun (which was mounted in the U.S. Army's M36 tank destroyer and M26 Pershing heavy tank). Compared to the American 76mm gun, the British gun had a longer barrel and far superior ammunition with a much larger propellant content.

Wisely, the British Army decided to start production of this new vehicle, sometimes known as the "Firefly," as soon as possible. As a result, the British Army had at least one Firefly in each of its tank troops (four tanks) by D-day. Three versions of the Firefly existed; the most numerous model derived from the first-generation M4A4, while lesser numbers were converted from the first-generation M4 and the later production first-generation M4 with the composite hull.

Since the British Army Firefly was one of the only Allied tanks at the beginning of the invasion of Europe

The mainstay of the North Korean armored force in the Korean War consisted of the T34/85 medium tank. In firepower, protection, and mobility, both the Russian and American M4A3(76)W HVSS were about equal in combat effectiveness. Due to the better training of American tank crews, they normally prevailed in head-on clashes between the two tanks. *Defense Visual Information Center*

that could punch holes in German late-war tanks, the U.S. Army sought to place 160 units of the vehicle into service as quickly as possible. A combination of factors, such as a temporary shortage of M4 series tank suitable for conversation, the British Army's own needs, and the fact that it was not an American-designed weapon all conspired to prevent it from entering service until after the war in Europe ended. Records show the U.S. Army had one hundred of the conversions armed with the 17-pounder completed and in the inventory at one point in time. With the reorientation of the U.S. Army for the planned invasion of Japan, the U.S. Army left its version of the Firefly behind. Their eventual fate remains unknown.

THE M4A3(76)W HVSS IN KOREA

The North Korean government promoted and supported an insurgency in South Korea in the late 1940s. When this failed, North Korea attacked in force on June 25, 1950, sending its army (led by T34/85 tanks) across the 38th parallel that divides Korea into separate countries.

In response, President Harry Truman—with the support of the United Nations (UN)—committed the U.S. military to the defense of South Korea. Since most of the U.S. Army equipment consisted of leftovers from World War II, the M4 series of tanks played an important role, first showing up in the country on July 31, 1950. While the Marine Corps had mostly the 105mm howitzer-equipped M4 series tank in service during the Korean conflict, the U.S. Army brought the M4A3(76)W HVSS to the fight among other types of tanks.

The following narrative, provided by the library staff from the U.S. Army Office of the Chief of Military History, provides a feel for M4A3(76)W HVSS performance during combat action during the early part of the Korean War:

The attack started with Lieutenant Nordstrom's tank in the lead. Within 100 yards of the road cut, Nordstrom noticed enemy soldiers hurriedly climbing the hill on the left of the road. He ordered his machine gunner to open fire on them. At about the

An M4A3(76)W HVSS tank is firing at enemy hilltop positions during the Korean War. The camouflage paint job was not common during this period. During the Korean War, the American military estimated that 70 percent of its tank losses were due to antitank mines. During World War II, losses of American tanks to mines was only about 20 percent. *Patton Museum*

same time he spotted an enemy machine-gun crew moving its gun toward the pass, and took these men under fire with the 76mm gun. The first shell struck the ground next to the enemy crew, and the burst blew away some foliage that was camouflaging an enemy tank dug in on the approach side of the pass on the right side of the road. As soon as the camouflage was disturbed, the enemy tank fired one round. The tracer passed between Nordstrom's head and the open hatch cover. In these circumstances he did not take time to give fire orders; he just called for armor-piercing shells and the gunner fired, hitting the front of the enemy tank from a distance of less than 100 yards. The gunner continued firing armor-piercing shells and the third round caused a great explosion. Ammunition and gasoline began to burn simultaneously. Black smoke drifted east and north across the high ground on the right side of the pass, effectively screening that area.

By the time of the Korean War, some M4A3(76)W HVSS tanks carried only HE main gun rounds and HVAP rounds, as is seen in this passage from a article titled, "Tankers at Heartbreak," which appeared in the September–October, 1952, issue of *Armor* magazine: "It was a vigorous, penetrating thrust, brilliantly planned and daringly executed. Every tanker in the battalion rode to the

attack in 68 Shermans loaded with HE and hyper-shot and carried extra ammunition for the battalion of the 38th Infantry marching along to nail the antitank squads."

The extreme close-quarter nature of the fighting in Korea as relates to the M4A3(76)W HVSS is evident from this extract from an article titled "Armor Holds the Hill" in the January–February 1953 issue of "Armor" magazine:

North Korean troops crawled up onto the tanks, blocking the vision devices, exploding shaped charges and attempting to jam the 76mm gun tube and plug the .30 caliber coaxial machine guns in an effort to silence the fire from the tanks. The tankers fired on one another, traversing their turrets to knock enemy troops from the decks. The fighting raged all night as the enemy reinforced the assault force to battalion size. Daylight on the 22nd revealed North Koreans all around the tank positions and in control of the hilltop. Friendly infantrymen had been forced off the crest, but the tanks held their ground. One Red [communist] soldier was observed firing the .50 caliber machine gun from the top of one of the tanks. He was shot off by friendly fire.

Back at the tank immobilized with a bad clutch, the situation grew steady worse. It was desperately engaged with the North Koreans when a bazooka round penetrated the turret, killing the tank commander. A medic who was in the tank opened the hatch but was killed by a burst from a burp gun [submachine gun]. Several North Koreans hand grenades then were lobbed into the open hatch but the remaining crew members managed to throw them out before they exploded and then succeeded in securing the hatch. The Reds fired several machine gun bursts at the hole caused by the bazooka, while inside the tank a crew member attempted to hold a helmet over the hole to stem the fire.

During the later stages of the Korean War, the targets for the 76mm gun on the M4A3(76)W HVSS were no longer enemy tanks, but elaborate enemy bunkers, as seen in this article titled "Bunker Destruction by Tank Cannon," which appeared in the March–April 1952 issue of *Armor* magazine:

After the natural growth or camouflage has been removed and the embrasure [firing port] exposed the next consideration is the prevention, or the stopping of fire from any weapon in the bunker. This is accomplished by the delivery of direct cannon fire into the embrasure itself. HE, fuse quick, is used initially, followed by a few rounds of HE, fuse delay, or WP to cause casualties among members of the enemy gun crew who may have withdrawn into the connecting tunnel or supply shelter. . . . When the enemy weapon has been silenced, the destruction of the bunker has begun. . . . The ammunition to be used is a combination of APC and HE fuse delay delivered as follows:

1. One or more rounds of APC directed immediately above the bunker embrasure followed by one or more rounds of HE fuse delay.

2. One or more rounds of APC directed three to five feet below the embrasure followed by one or more rounds of HE fuse delay.

The process follows the principle of the "pick and shovel." The APC traveling at terrific speed smashes into the roof and floor, loosens the earth, and logs. The following HE blows the loosened material downward and upward along the path of least resistance, the gun chamber.

The Korean War would drag on until July 1953 before an armistice came about that ended the armed phase of the conflict. By that time, the M26 Pershing (now classified as a medium tank) and an improved model designated the M46 Patton—also armed with a 90mm main gun—began to appear in greater numbers.

What did the American tankers think of the M46 Patton tank compared to the M4A3(76)W HVSS? A partial answer is provided in a short article under a section titled "Sum and Substance," written by Sergeant Dale A. Mille and published in the September–October 1952 issue of *Armor* magazine: "Driving the M46 in combat after training in an M4 is like stepping from a Model T Ford into a new Cadillac. . . . I think the M46 is a dream to drive compared with the old M4. You can drive all day and not become tired. And that means a lot when you have long missions over rough terrain and need to be on your toes in enemy action or watching for mines."

Already in production during the Korean War was the replacement for both the M26 Pershing tank and the M46 Patton tank. It would appear as the M47 Patton tank. These new, better-armed and -armored tanks would push the M4A3(76)W HVSS out of frontline service and into the U.S. Army National Guard and Reserves, where some would go on to serve into the early 1970s.

Those remaining M4 series tanks of the first and second generations to have survived military service in American or foreign military service and the target ranges, now reside in military museums around the world or in the hands of private collectors—restored to running condition, minus the operational weapons.

At some point in the Korean War, the belief arose in some quarters of the U.S. Army that by painting tiger faces on the front of their M4A3(76)W HVSS tanks, the uneducated and superstition Chinese troops would be cowed in inaction. Many might have questioned the validity of this belief; however, the tankers no doubt enjoyed the chance to personify their tanks, as the crew of this vehicle is proudly showing off to the camera operator. *Patton Museum*

INDEX

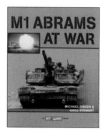

M1 Abrams at War
ISBN 0-7603-2153-1

Panzers at War
ISBN 0-7603-2152-3

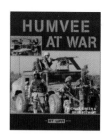

Humvee at War
ISBN 0-7603-2151-5

**German Tanks of
World War II in Color**
ISBN 0-7603-0671-0

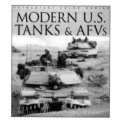

Modern Tanks and AFVs
ISBN 0-7603-1467-5

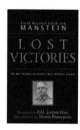

Lost Victories
ISBN 0-7603-2054-3

Blitzkrieg: In Their Own Words
ISBN 0-7603-2186-8

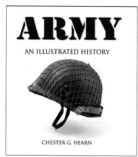

Army: An Illustrated History
ISBN 0-7603-2680-0

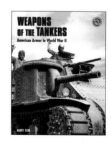

Weapons of the Tankers
ISBN 0-7603-2329-1